Initiation into the Philosophy
of
Plato

This book was originally published in Italian as, *Iniziazione alla Filosofia di Platone*, Edizioni Āśram Vidyā, Roma.

First Published in English in 1999 by
Shepheard-Walwyn (Publishers) Ltd.
London, England

Revised English Edition in 2005 by
The Aurea Vidyā Foundation, Inc.
325 Canal Street, New York, N.Y. 10013, U.S.A.
www.vidya-ashramvidyaorder.org

©Āśram Vidyā 1984
©Āśram Vidyā 1996 Second Edition
English Translation ©Āśram Vidyā 1999 and 2005

Set in font ©Vidyā 11/13 points by Aurea Vidyā

Printed and bound in the U.S.A.
by Sheridan Books, Ann Arbor, Michigan

The revenues from the sale of this book, for which there are no copyright obligations to the Author, will be used for reprints.

ISBN   1-931406-07-3
Library of Congress Control Number: 2005904413

On the cover: «Socrates»
                  Reproduction by kind permission of,
                  DAI - Roma, (Inst. Neg. Nr. 36.896) and,
                  Museo Archeologico - Napoli.

Raphael

Initiation into the Philosophy
of
Plato

AUREA VIDYĀ

TABLE OF CONTENTS

Beauty is the splendour of Truth.

Plato

A full and proper relationship with
Truth cannot but produce Good.

Raphael

FOREWORD

We will no doubt have heard many references to Plato's philosophy from philosophers, historians, philologists, even from friends and neighbours who may have heard of it or studied it at University.

So much has been written about Plato in so many of the world's principal languages that, according to Professor G. Reale, it is almost impossible to digest all the literature that exists concerning him. It is easy to understand, therefore, why for some time now a number of scholars have suggested dispensing with all this literature and proceeding to read Plato without its mediation or in some way independently. Besides, each commentator expresses a view of his own which, at times, contradicts that of others. Such, for example, is the case with the many different interpretations which have been proposed for concepts such as *philía, Eros, demiurge, chóra*, etc.

However much may have been read or even studied, very few indeed have actually *meditated* deeply on Platonic Teaching without scholarly preconceptions, grasping its essence and its profound ascetic and realizational content.

What is meant here by the term "ascetic" is a "raising", a "turning" of the consciousness from the sensible to the suprasensible. Plato's is, therefore, a philosophy of catharsis, ascent, realization, transformation of the way of feeling, of willing, of acting. Plato uses philosophy as a method for raising us above the conflict-ridden and contradictory world of the sensible to the harmonious world of Being, which is our original home.

Over the centuries the concept of philosophy has assumed a completely different meaning from the original one, to the extent that it has become a mere "mental game", an arid conceptual exercise involving the products of the empirical, phenomenal and imaginative mind which can offer only *opinions*, not Truth.

Plato's philosophy is of an *initiatory order*, it is conversion to Being, it is Initiation into the supreme Good - and this is not our idea but Plato's.

Thus, in order to comprehend it, it is not sufficient to discuss and mentally elaborate it; one must integrate it in one's consciousness. In other words, one must realize it and live it. It is by absorbing it into our consciousness that we can find the answers to so many apparently unsolvable questions and discover truths which might at first sight appear irrational.

Platonism was taken into consideration also by the Islamic philosophers (Avicenna, etc.) readers of the hellenic masters and even by the Church Fathers (Ambrose, Augustine, Giovanni Damasciano and Anselm of Canterbury, amongst others) and continued to be approved by the Church until the twelfth century.

The Renaissance gave it a positive impulse with, in Florence, the Academy of Marsilio Ficino[1] (Pico della Mirandola, Poliziano *et al*); and, in England, the Cambridge Platonists (Henry More, Theophilus Gale, John Norris, *et al*).

---

[1] Cp. *Letters of Marsilio Ficino*, Shepheard-Walwyn, London.

Though the Platonic Academy in Athens was shut by Justinian in 529 A.D., in fact Platonism never died, and there have always been groups and single individuals who have meditated upon it, realized it and expressed it.

Platonic philosophy is characterized by a profound aspiration towards a different and better society, by a vision of life which includes man in his wholeness and not in his phenomenal and sensory fragmentation. It favours a method of study that requires gradual apprehension by the intellect rather than the use of formal logic; but its chief characteristic is its firm conviction of man's ability to *comprehend* and realize noetic Truth and to model his life and the objectives of life upon this principle of truth.

Plato revealed a traditional initiatory Teaching which must be considered "sacred", and those who seek Platonic philosophical Initiation must approach it with this in mind. We can say that what Plato and Platonism offer to the West is nothing less than a traditional pathway of self-realization of a metaphysical order. To this day those who have the proper qualifications can gain access to it.

In these pages Raphael offers only an introduction to Platonic teaching, leaving to the student the task of direct *meditation* on the texts.

Besides offering many quotations of contemporary Authors who validate the thesis presented in this writing, Raphael also draws a brief comparison between Plato and Śaṅkara, the codifier of the *Advaita Vedānta* of Vedic inspiration.

These two Teachings, codified by divine Masters, may appear to be far removed from one another and very different, but anyone who has realized that there is only one universal Tradition of the Mysteries can easily see how they are only "adaptations" dictated by time and space.

Those who are able to approach these Teachings sacredly may derive proper benefit from them and eventually attain philosophical catharsis (*metánoia-periagogé*, μετάνοια-περιαγωγή)[1].

---

[1] Cp. *Politéia*, VII, 518 b - 519 b.

Notes:

1. The Greek term *Politéia* is usually translated as "Republic", though its meaning is closer to "Constitution", as it applies to all forms of state organization. We have chosen to keep the term *Politéia* to convey this far broader meaning.

2. Quotations along the text from Plato's and Plotinus' works have been directly translated from the following Italian editions:

Platone, *Tutte le Opere*, Sansoni, Firenze.

Platone, *Tutti gli scritti*, Rusconi, Milano.

Platone, *I Dialoghi*, Rizzoli, Milano.

Platone, *Cratilo*, Laterza, Bari

Plotino, *Enneadi*, Laterza, Bari.

3. For the meaning of some Greek and Sankrit terms please refer to the "Glossary" on page 153.

But I do not think that a discussion of these topics is good for men, except for the few who are able, after a few indications, to find truth by themselves; as regards the others, some of them would simply become puffed up with unjustified disdain, which is not good, others with pride and vain confidence, as if they had learnt something sublime.

Plato, *Letter VII*, 341

Teaching does not go beyond the limit of pointing out the way and the journey; but the vision is totally the personal task of those who have resolved to contemplate.

Plotinus, *Enneads*, VI, 9, IV

THE SPHERE OF BEING OR OF IDEAS

Plato was born in Athens in 428 B.C. in the month of Thargelion (May-June) into an ancient and noble family. Originally he was known as Aristocle. His father Ariston was descended from the last kings of Athens and directly from the mythical king Codrus, and his mother Perictione, through Critias, was descended from Dropide of the house of Solon.

As a youth he observed the great political events and upheavals which caused Athens to lose its hegemony over Greece (the Peloponnesian War).

It seems that some members of his family may have been influential members of the aristocratic party, and it is even believed that Plato himself took part in the so-called "government of the thirty" which came to power in 404 B.C. However - as Plato himself informs us - disgusted by the ingrained pettiness, selfishness, injustice and arrogance of his party, as well as of the democratic party, he retired from the political scene convinced that only philosopher rulers or reigning philosophers - that is to say, persons who had achieved true interior catharsis - could solve the problems and ills of society. Such was the impact of the "misery of politics" and the improper relationship between the rulers and the ruled on him that he contemplated and conceived an "Ideal State", a state whose principles were inspired by the world of Ideas, or by the metaphysical Idea-Archetype of the state.

He was introduced to philosophy by Cratylus, a disciple of Heraclitus, whose philosophy rests upon *becoming* rather than on Being. But the person who had the most lasting and important influence upon him was Socrates whose faithful and attentive follower he was for many years. And it was Socrates who became the protagonist of his dialogues.

When Socrates died in 399 B.C., Plato went on a series of journeys for about ten years: he went to Egypt, where he was initiated into the Egyptian mysteries; to the south of Italy and to Tarentum where he came into contact with Archytas, the leader of the Pythagoreans of the area; towards the year 390 B.C. he went to Syracuse in Sicily to the court of the tyrant Dionysius the Elder in the hope of setting up the Ideal State.

He did not succeed either with the elder Dionysius or with the Younger, who succeeded him. Plato therefore returned to Athens and devoted himself entirely to Philosophy, founding the Academy as a training ground for philosophical debate and "dialectics". In 347 B.C. he abandoned his "mortal shadow-sheath" to fly towards the world of pure Ideas or of Being.

We may say that the Platonic Academy was of a sacred nature, headed by a Scholarch whose term of office lasted until death. The Scholarch not only looked after the general running of the organization, but was also in charge of sacrificial functions, ritual convivia, and so on.

* * *

«The essence of Platonism, writes Domenico Pesce, lies in a radical reversing of the common perception of reality and of life. Where the common man sees the very nature of being as solid corporeal objects, believes he has truly understood an event when he is able to explain it as being the necessary outcome of a foregoing event, identifies knowledge with seeing and touching and considers good as being nothing but pleasant experiences, Plato counters this ingenuous materialism with the strong conviction that truly real is only what reveals itself as simple and unchanging, that is, the invisible and intangibile spiritual substance; he rejects mechanistic thinking by stating that the material antecedent, as it is unable to explain why a certain effect rather than another is produced, explains nothing, because the true cause must instead be sought in the intelligible, and therefore meaningful, form which case by case manifests itself on the material plane; lastly he vigorously rebuts sensationalism and hedonism, stating that true knowledge is achieved not by turning towards the external but towards the internal, that it resides in the depth of the soul and that true goodness should be pursued by renouncing earthly pleasure, by flying away from the sensible world and by aspiring towards the death [of the empirical ego]»[1].

On the basis of this premise we can see that Plato posits a distinction - but not an absolute opposition - between

---

[1] Domenico Pesce, *Il pensiero neoplatonico*, La Nuova Italia Editrice, Firenze 1961. [Italian edition].

the intelligible, permanent and incorruptible world and the sensible, fleeting and corruptible one. This recognition of the suprasensible and of the constant represents for Plato the "second navigation".

But the "second navigation" (δεύτερος πλοῦς, *Phaedo*, 99) cannot be understood by letting oneself be guided by the sensible mind, which offers one only opinions, but by the noetic mind (*noûs*).

Plato writes: «Upon this there is not, nor will there ever be, a treatise by me because this discipline, unlike others, is absolutely impossible to *communicate*. But after many discussions on this problem and a long time spent dwelling on it, suddenly, like a light coming from a spark, it is born in the soul and it feeds of itself... But I do not think that a discussion of these topics is good for men, except for the few who are able, after a few indications, to find truth by themselves; as regards the others, some of them would simply become puffed up with unjustified disdain, which is not good, others with pride and vain confidence, as if they had learnt something sublime»[1].

Plato's doctrine - like that of Śaṅkara, the codifier of *Advaita Vedānta*, with which we shall make a comparison - belonging as it does to the Great Mysteries, is not aimed at the selective and representative empirical mind, or at the "ego" of phenomena, but at the Soul, at the *noûs* (νοῦς).

This "second navigation" thus leads to the recognition of two planes of Being: the one intelligible, metempirical, suprasensible and accessible only to the noetic mind; the other phenomenal, visible to the senses. The former is that of Being, the latter that of becoming. These represent different levels of manifestation.

---

[1] Plato, *Letter VII*, 341. Op. cit.

We read in the *Politéia*:

«Do you wish us to examine first this question?　And that is, how are these characters formed, how can they be elevated into the light, as some are said to have been raised up from Hades and brought amid the Gods?
- How could one not so wish?　he said.
- So, as it would appear, we are not merely talking of turning a tile face up, but of the total turning away (περιαγωγή) of the Soul from darkness to full daylight, an ascent, that is towards Being; which, according to us, is the task of the true philosopher.
- Without doubt.
- Must we not, therefore, investigate which of the disciplines has this power?
- Why not?
- Well, Glaucon, which of the disciplines might succeed in raising the Soul up from the world of becoming to that of Being?　And in saying this I ask myself:　did we not state that these philosophers of ours needed to be athletes from their youth?
... And so, when one, by the use of dialectics, without the help of the senses, by means of the intellect, tries to attain to the knowledge of each being in itself and does not give up on his investigation before having grasped what is the Good in itself, he comes thus to the contemplation of the intelligible, in the same way as the other fellow comes to the contemplation of the visible»[1].

Plato gives exoteric expression to a fundamental principle of the Teaching of the Mysteries as earlier expounded by Orpheus, that of the intelligibility of one part of us.　With Plato there is a clear and manifest distinction between imma-

---

[1] Plato, *Politéia*, VII, 521 and 532. Op. cit.

nence and transcendence, between spirit and matter, between the sensible and the suprasensible, between the relative and the absolute. But this duality, as we shall see, for him, for the Teaching of the Mysteries, for the whole of the Initiatory Tradition, is not absolute.

The followers of Orphism considered the Soul (of the intelligible order) as being enclosed within the body (of the sensible order), which, like all bodies, represents a "tomb", a "prison"; the task of the being is to rise from this "tomb" and awaken to the recognition of its own immortality. It is necessary «to raise the Soul up from the world of becoming to that of Being».

The Tradition - which, we must always remember, is not of a human order - is not nihilist because it does not consider being as perishable, mortal and restricted by the dualism of the senses; furthermore, it indicates a way by which we may emerge from the "tomb" and grow the wings required to attain the dimension of freedom. Plato follows this Tradition, extending the reality of man beyond the limits of the concrete and sensorial, with all its conflicts, restoring him thus to the universal dimension and giving him back his raison d'être.

The suprasensible, or the intelligible, is characterized by the "world of Ideas", while the sensible world is composed of *copies*, of prototypes, mere imitations of the Ideas. For Plato there is one Reality: Being or the world of Ideas. All the rest - rather than being a nothing - are simply as accurate images as possible of the Ideas.

An analogy might be the following: all the external creations of the individual are simply prototypes, copies conforming as accurately as may be to his ideas and thoughts. Each object is nothing but an idea or a thought materialized. But the idea and the object do not represent a duality; the object is only an effect, a phenomenon, an accidental thing which is born and which dies; if in this specific case one were to seek Reality, one would be obliged to recognize the fact that only the idea, which survives the destructibility of the object, is real. But Plato's Idea is not the same as that of man's thinking.

The entire sensible world with its numberless expressive possibilities (the names and forms of *Vedānta*) is an objectified reflection of a reality, the only Reality, which is the world of Ideas.

For the benefit of those who are not familiar with Platonic philosophy, let us now make a few clarifying remarks concerning the term Idea.

The term "idea" is derived from the Greek ἰδέα and εἶδος, but unfortunately this word gives rise to misunderstandings because it may indicate a number of things. Essentially it has three meanings: first, an essence, substance, form or species of universal order: they are ontological concepts which might be compared to pure spirit; second, a mental content in the general sense, representing principally a psychological aspect: this is the image which we normally have of the term idea; third, the image of a project synthesized in an idea.

Plato, with other Greek philosophers, uses the term idea in its first meaning. For example, Democritus' atom is ἰδέα, it is a universal entity. Therefore, the Platonic Idea is not a concept, a thought, a mental representation, it is not a psychological datum; according to Plato these data are simply "shadows", opinions. The Idea is the metaphysical basis of all that exists and *is*; it is the ontological structure-essence of all things. The Idea is an intelligible datum without which the sensible world could not exist. The Idea is Being insofar as it *is* and does not become, it is the constant upon which becoming rests, it is the central sun around which all sensible things revolve, it is the *arché*, the principle on which all entities depend. To indicate this Idea Plato also uses the term ουσία, that is essence, substance.

It is necessary, therefore, to make a clearcut distinction between the ideal world of human and psychological thinking and Plato's "ideal world". There is another aspect to consider. One could say that each of Plato's commentators has given his own interpretation; this is due in part to the fact that Plato's is not a systematic, absolutist, univocal philosophy, and therefore gives rise to as many points of view as there are mental positions. In fact so much has been written about Plato and his Doctrine from different and opposing points of view that it could easily fill a library of considerable proportions. This does not mean that there is not a straight-forward and coherent basis of teaching, a deep, unitary doctrinal nucleus underlying the philosophy of Plato. Indeed, it is that very traditional nucleus that we are focusing on here. As long as the empirical, relational mind is interpreting the philosopher of Athens, there are bound to be innumerable, even contrasting and discordant, interpretations. If, however, it is the intuitive, noetic mind which interprets him, things change.

As far as the "doctrine of Ideas" is concerned the situation does not change, in fact we have a great number of interpretative concepts which, when all is said and done, remain mere concepts. This is equally true of Plato's Eros, and so on.

One thing is certain, however: that the "mysticism" of the Ideas is fundamental to the philosophy of Plato, and failure to grasp this basic fact can lead one far astray.

Plato's is a *Philosophy of Being*: the part concerning the One-Good as metaphysical Being is of an esoteric nature and in the Academy it was approached only by members possessing adequate receptive capacities.

The theory of Ideas has caused a certain degree of confusion especially on account of its interpretation by Aristotle. The Stagirite conceived the Ideas from his own point of view and not from that of Plato. This is a fact that has now been verified by many interpreters of Plato.

Reale, for example, tries to clarify the theory of Ideas on the basis of Plato's own writings. Here is what he writes: «Let us begin with the character of *perseity* attributed to the Ideas: the Ideas are repeatedly stated as being "in themselves" and "in and by themselves". Indeed Plato uses the expression "in itself" as synonymous with "Idea", and instead of the Idea of beauty, the Idea of good, etc., he speaks about Beauty-in-itself, Good-in-itself and so on. This expression has often been interpreted (following Aristotle) in its hypostatic meaning, as if it clearly revealed the Idea as nothing other than the ontological form of a concept or the entification of an abstract, the hypostatization of the universal. But this expression has a quite different meaning in the Platonic context. Plato, we note, gradually developed and established his theory of Ideas *in opposition to two closely connected forms of relativism*: a) that of the Sophists and Protagoreans, who reduced all reality and action to something purely subjective and made the subject itself the measure or *criterion of the truth* of all things; b) that of the Heraclitans who, by proclaiming the eternal flow and radical mobility of all things, ended up fragmenting every thing into an irreducible multiplicity of relative states, thereby rendering everything fleeting, unknowable, unintelligible. Pondering over these two forms of relativism, Plato comprehended and established the fundamental character of Ideas, as *in itself*. Thus the meaning of the statement that the Idea is *in itself* and *by itself* is clear. It means that things have an essence that is not *relative* to the subject, that refuses to be manipulated at the whim of the subject: i.e. the essence or the nature or Idea of things is *absolute*. If this were not so, every judgement of ours (regarding anything whatsoever, and in particular all our moral judgements) would be devoid of significance and our discourse would be meaningless. Therefore the *in itself* and *by itself* indicates the absoluteness (non-relativity) of the Ideas. But, as this is an extremely important aspect of the Ideas and as, furthermore, it has been seriously misunderstood, it is opportune to read Plato's revealing words on the matter»[1].

The *perseity* of Ideas contradicts the Sophistic-Protagorean relativism; Plato maintains:

«Socrates - Well now, let us see, Hermogenes, if you hold that even for the entities it is thus: that their essence is relative to each of us individually, as Protagoras claimed, saying that "the measure of all things" is man; so that, as things appear to be to me, so they are for me, and as they appear to be to you, so they are for you? Or do you believe that things *have a permanent essence of their own*?

Hermogenes - There was a time, Socrates, when, finding myself in doubt, I was drawn to what Protagoras maintains; but I do not really believe that things are thus.

Socrates - And so you let yourself be drawn to believe this, that there exists no such thing as a *bad man*?

Hermogenes - Certainly not! indeed I have more than once found to my expense that bad men do exist, and a good many of them too.

---

[1] G. Reale, *Storia della Filosofia antica*, vol. II. Vita e Pensiero. Milano. [Italian edition]. E. T., *A History of Ancient Philosophy*, SUNY Press, Albany 1985 ss.

Socrates - And have you ever believed that there are men who are wholly good?

Hermogenes - Yes, but very few.

Socrates - In any case you have believed that good men existed.

Hermogenes - Yes.

Socrates - Well now, how do you understand this? Perhaps thus, that men who are wholly good are utterly wise, and that those who are wholly bad are completely devoid of wisdom?

Hermogenes - So it appears to me.

Socrates - Is it possible then, if Protagoras was speaking truly and it is indeed the case that, as things appear to each of us to be, so they are in reality, that some of us may be wise and others not?

Hermogenes - No, indeed not.

Socrates - Surely you will admit this too, I believe, that if there is wisdom and foolishness it is not possible that Protagoras speaks truly, because no man can in truth be wiser than another if each of us believes that only what appears to him to be true is true.

Hermogenes - That is so.

Socrates - But you will not, I think, agree with Euthydemos either, according to whom all things are, entirely and at all times, the same for everybody; because, in this case, men could not be some of them good, and others bad, if all of them at all times had vices and virtues in equal measure.

Hermogenes - This is true.

Socrates - If all things are not the same to all men entirely and at all times, and if each thing is not particular and peculiar to each man, it is clear that the things themselves must contain in themselves their own permanent essence. They do not depend upon us, nor are they pulled up or down by our imagination, but they exist by themselves, according to their own essence, as they are by nature»[1].

The *perseity* of the Ideas also argues against Heraclitus' concept of impermanence:

«Socrates - So that the many names that tend towards the same point may not confound us, we must investigate the following: if in reality those who imposed the names did so in the conviction that all things move constantly and flow - and it appears to me too that they were convinced of this - or if, by chance, this is not so, and they, drawn and carried away as if by a vortex, drag us and throw us into it too. Consider, therefore, my excellent Cratylus, what I often muse upon. Do we or do we not say that there is beauty in itself, goodness in itself, and equally so for each being?

Cratylus - It seems so to me, Socrates.

Socrates - Let us consider therefore this beauty in itself; not whether a face is beautiful or whether some other object of the same type is beautiful - things, that is, that seem to flow; and let us see: does this beauty in itself remain identical to itself or does it not?

Cratylus - It must necessarily remain so.

Socrates - Well then, is it possible that this beauty be appropriately called beauty in itself, if it is always, first as to being and then as to being this or that, escaping from our grasp? or is it not necessarily the case that, in the very moment that we enounce it (due to its transitory nature)

---

[1] Plato, *Cratylus*, 385 e - 386 e. Op. cit. The translation has been correlated to the one of Martini's.

it becomes something else and escapes from us and is no longer what it was?

Cratylus - It must of necessity (flee from us, in accordance with its specific nature).

Socrates - Then how can something be if it is not always the same? Because if for just one moment it stands still and the same, it is clear that at least in that moment it cannot pass, and if it always remains the same, how could it change or move without any departure from its idea?

Cratylus - It could not do so at all.

Socrates - But then it could not be known by anyone either. In fact, the very moment it has to be known and one draws near, it becomes different and of another species, and it can no longer be known as it is or for what it is. No knowledge would, surely, be possible if that which is to be known did not in any way stand still.

Cratylus - It is as you say»[1].

In this passage from *Phaedo* Plato is still carrying on a controversy with Heraclitus' theory of becoming:

«The Being in itself, which we strive to define by question and answer, does remain always identical to itself or does it change from time to time? Can the equal in itself, Beauty in itself, that which each thing is in itself, in other words Being, ever admit even the slightest change to take place? Namely each of these absolute realities, being uniform in itself, is always identical to itself, and never admits in any way or manner any change whatever?

Cebes - It is necessary, Socrates, he said, for it to remain ever the same identical to itself.

- What then shall we say of such things as men, horses, garments, and indeed of all other things, equal or beauti-

---

[1] *Ibid.*, 439 b - 440 a. Op. cit.

ful or distinct by names derived from those essences? Are these, perhaps, always identical to themselves or, contrary to those, are they in no way ever the same either with relation to themselves or in relation to each other?

- Exactly, said Cebes, they are never the same»[1].

Thus, the world of names and forms changes, and the things of the senses change but what determines the change cannot change. We can say that Being is the metaphysical foundation of becoming, of the phenomenal, of that "appearance" of which Parmenides speaks. Becoming participates in the reality of Being but is not Being, as a strand of hair participates in the reality of a being but is not that being as such.

Furthermore, the Ideas are conceived by Plato as absolute Being (τὸ ὄν). Being, in that it is and cannot become, cannot find itself to be anything but itself, cannot cease to be, because it would in such case not be a Being what it is. In this context Plato relates back to Parmenides[2].

Let us also read how the Neoplatonist Plotinus expounds the concept of Spirit-Being:

«Let it therefore be firmly established that Spirit is Being in its plurality: It holds all things within itself not as if in a place but by virtue of the fact that it possesses itself and is one with them. But up there all beings are together and, nevertheless, they are separate. And even the Soul, although it holds within itself all the sciences at once, presents no

---

[1] Plato, *Phaedo*, 78d - 79a.Op.cit.

[2] On Parmenides' "vision" cp. Raphael, *The Pathway of Non-duality*. Edizioni Āśram Vidyā, Roma. [Italian edition]. English edition by Motilal Banarsidass, Delhi.

confusion; rather, each science carries out its own specific task when asked to do so, without involving the others, and even the idea acts by itself, singularly, without mixing with the other ideas which dwell there on their own.

Thus, and indeed to a far greater extent, the Spirit is "all beings" *together* and, on the other hand, not together, since each being is a particular force; but the Spirit on the whole embraces all things as a genus does the species and the whole its parts. The forces of the seed as well offer us an image of what I am speaking about: in the whole seed, I mean, all is present in an indistinct state and the formal reasons are there as in a single centre. There is one formal reason for the eye and a different one for the hands; the "different" is recognized only by way of the sense organ generated by it.

Now, as far as the forces enclosed in the seed are concerned, each one of these represents a formal, unitary and total reason with the parts it itself embraces. However, while a corporeal part has matter - all that in the seed is humidity, for example - the force in itself, as such, is instead form in its totality and, precisely, rational form which identifies with a certain kind of soul - the generating soul - which, in turn, is an image of another superior soul. Some call "nature" that soul which operates in seeds; departed from up high, from that which pre-existed to it, like light from fire, it transmutes and configures matter not through a mechanical thrust or by applying levers, which are so highly praised at present, but by simply making it participate in the formal reasons»[1].

---

[1] Plotinus, *Enneads*, V, 9, VI. For the plurality of the Ideas in the unity of Being see also, *Enneads* VI. Op. cit.

THE ONE-GOOD AS METAPHYSICAL REALITY

Ideas are manifold, although they are expressions of Unity-Being, and are organized hierarchically: on the lowest level of the hierarchy are the Ideas of the geometrical-mathematical entities, on the higher level, the Ideas of ethical and aesthetic values; Plato, however, in his *Politéia* (510, 511), speaks of an *unconditioned principle* which is beyond the world of Ideas itself, that is, beyond Being or Essence. This Supreme Good is the One-One which is the root of the world of Ideas which, in its turn, is the One-many, while the sensible constitutes the One *and* the many.

In his *Statesman* Plato says expressly:

«For all this, therefore, one can neither say that the world always conducts itself by itself alone nor, vice-versa, that it is entirely conducted by the divinity in two opposite directions; nor, indeed, that it is conducted by two Gods each animated by a thought contrary to that of the other»[1].

Another dialogue in which Plato expresses the same concept is in the *Politéia*:

«Therefore, That which conveys truth to knowable objects and the power to know them to him who knows them, you can certainly say is the Idea of the Good. And while you must think of it as cause of knowledge and truth, insofar as this is known, also, because both truth and knowledge are

---

[1] Plato, *Statesman*, XIII, 269. Op. cit.

beautiful things, if you maintain that the Idea of the Good is distinct from them and is even more beautiful, you will be in no way mistaken.

And just as in the sensible world light and sight resemble the sun, but is not right to take them for the sun, similarly in the intelligible world it is right to hold that knowledge and truth are both similar to the Good, but it is not right to hold that either of them is the Good, the nature of which must rather be considered as far more precious.

- You attribute to it, he said, insurmountable beauty, if it is the source of cognition and of truth, and exceeds them in beauty; but to be sure, it is not of pleasure that you intend to talk about.

- Certainly not! I exclaimed, but consider even better the image of the Good in this way.

- Yes, how?

- Of the sun, I think you can say that it gives to visible objects not only the faculty of being seen, but also generation, growth and nourishment, without itself being generation.

- Without any doubt.

- And so you can say that knowable things do not derive from the Good only their knowability, but also their existence and their essence, although *the Good is not essence, but in dignity and power is even above Essence*»[1].

And again:

«...But I believe it to be thus: that in the intelligible world the Idea of the Good is the highest and the most difficult to discern; but once it is discerned one must conclude that it is for all the cause of everything good and beautiful, in fact in the visible world it has generated the light and its

---

[1] Plato, *Politéia*, VI, 508-509. Op. cit. [Italics ours].

Lord, and in the intelligible world, where it equally rules, it has produced truth and intelligence...»[1].

This passage is very important because it enables one to comprehend that the sensible-intelligible polarity depends upon the sovereign Idea of the Good. It is evident, therefore, that the supreme Idea of the Good, or the One-Good, is the cause of the entire manifestation at its various levels of Being, of knowability and of non-being. The One-Good is wherever the centre, never the circumference. It is the *unum supra ens*. Thus the *Esse* is not the supreme principle, but above it is the *Unum* or the *Bonum*. The supreme Good is species while Being is genus, it is "name", and it does not qualify the Totality, but only a determined moment of it.

It is important to point out that the Good of which we are talking about is not to be taken in a moral sense; the Good of Plato, and of Greek philosophy, is the supreme Intelligible, it is the supreme Ruler, the highest Knowledge (*Politéia*: VI 504a - 505b), the Measure of all things; it is Reality *par excellence*, that which gives life to the Intelligible itself and to Intelligence; it is the ultimate and metaphysical foundation of Being in its totality and of becoming. In the unwritten teachings it is called One-One.

Let us read also how Neoplatonism, embodied by Plotinus, expounds the concept of the Good or the One:

«...but Spirit (Being) can simply see either the things that precede it or the things that belong to it or the things that from its very self proceed. The things that are within it are already pure; but even purer and simpler are the things that precede it, or more precisely, the Only that precedes it. It is, therefore, not Spirit but is anterior to Spirit. Because Spirit is already "something" that falls within the beings.

---

[1] *Ibid.* VII, 517.

That One, on the contrary, is not "something" but is prior to every thing and is not even Being, because Being possesses, so to speak, a form, the form of Being, while That is non-formal, devoid, that is, even of spiritual form».

«...from which it follows that Plato is aware that from the Good derives the Spirit (Idea) and from the Spirit, the Soul...».

«[The Good], therefore, is not "something", not quality or quantity, not Spirit, nor Soul; it is not even to be found in "movement" nor, on the other hand, "in stillness"; it is not in a "space", it is not in a "time"; it is, instead, the solitary Ideal, entirely enclosed within itself or, rather, the Non-formal which pre-exists any ideal, which is prior to motion and prior to stillness because these values adhere to Being and make it manifold».

«But since we claim (and one may well believe it) that this Most High is everywhere and yet nowhere...»

«But the way out is denied to us above all because knowledge of Him cannot be obtained either by means of science or of thought, as in the case of the remaining objects of the Spirit, but only by means of a presence that is worth far more than science. Indeed, the Soul experiences separation from its own unity and does not remain completely one, as soon as it acquires scientific knowledge of something; science, in fact, is a logical process, but a logical process is multiplicity. Thus it departs from unity, because it has fallen into number and into multiplicity. It is therefore urgent to pass science quickly by and never deviate from our unitary being; it is necessary to abandon both science and the knowable as well as all other manifestation however beautiful, because any beauty is posterior to Him and derives from Him as the light of day totally derives from the sun. This is why of Him one cannot speak or write, as it has been said. Meanwhile we speak and write directing to Him, *to awaken from the sleep of words and into the awareness of vision*, nearly as to point out the way to those who wish to contemplate a little.

Frankly, the teaching does not extend beyond this limit, of pointing out the way and the journey; but the vision is indeed wholly a personal doing of he who resolved to contemplate»[1].

The idea of the One is not a vision that is merely abstract, theoretical or logical, nor a position of intellectual order, it rather implies the integral presence of all the dimensions of the spirit in a consciousness knowing. In Platonic thinking there is always a request for ascent and transcendence imposed by the restlessness and discontentment experienced by man, immersed in the finiteness of the sensible. Life tends towards reconquering that realm of *pax profunda* in accordance with the unequivocal aspiration of the human spirit.

Plato follows a traditional mysteric line, and we are certain that many things have not been said, while others have been conceptualized to satisfy the empirical minds of those disciples and of non-initiated otherwise unable to raise themselves up to a pure and simple contemplation of the Intelligible. The solution to many problems that were raised in some of the dialogues was not given, leaving it up to the disciple's research, meditation and intuition. Further, in order to make the Doctrine easier to accept and comprehend, He had the ingenious idea of formulating it in terms of dialogues; in fact he was the very first to present philosophy in a truly novel manner.

In any case, one notices that several tragedies of the same period exist whose content is profoundly esoteric.

---

[1] Plotinus, *Enneads*, VI, 9, III; V, 1, VIII; VI, 9, III; VI, 8, XVI; VI 9, IV. Op. cit. [Italics ours].

And now a very important question arises: did Plato have a true grasp of the real *metaphysical infinite*, or did his infinite represent only what the philosophers of ancient Greece called the *indefinite, the unlimited, indeterminate multiplicity*, etc.?

The unlimited, the indefinite, has a relative meaning, it is a passive, chaotic entity; it is that which, because of its finiteness, may be subject to enlargement, contraction, division, addition or multiplication (the great-small, the plus-minus). In fact, for Plato, the Idea, which is measure, truth and beauty, intervenes to make this *cháos*-unlimited a *cosmos*-limited which, for the Greek philosopher, is the expression of order, of harmony, of the right mathematical and geometrical proportions.

For the Greeks in general the infinite, or rather the unlimited-indeterminate, was a negative concept, a non-being. Aristotle, in fact, identifies it with the pure negativity of potential matter which is the opposite of that which has form-principle.

Certainly, the validity of all this is on the level of manifestation, at whatever dimension or degree one wants to conceive it. "Matter", as such, is indeterminate, is devoid of *logos*, of form; therefore it is irrational. It is exactly on this irrational matter that the Intelligence intervenes to provide order, that is number and quality. In fact, matter is wanting, it is privation, according to Aristotle; that which gives it life and foundation is the metaphysical Unity, which is transcendent but also immanent.

Plato sets out three levels of "entities" that account for the production of the universe, plus a fourth that governs them and which is their cause.

«First, then, is the unlimited; second the limit, and third that which is generated by their combination; and, finally, would I in some way strike the wrong note if I indicated as fourth the cause of combination and of generation?

Protarch - And how?...

Socrates - But it is easy, since all the learned, actually exalting themselves, agree that *the intellect (noûs) is for us the king of heaven and earth...*

... And so, is it your wish that we too should agree with this point, *as admitted by our predecessors*: i.e., that things are indeed this way, and that not only we believe we can repeat without danger the words of others, but also face the danger together with them and share in the risk and in the blame, should able men, highly skilful in dispute, state that these things are not thus but even that they are without order?

Protarch - And how could I not wish it?...

Socrates - Because for sure, Protarch, we cannot believe that of these four types - the limit, the unlimited, the combination and the cause - this fourth, *which is inherent in all things*, also because it gives to all living things both a soul and the use of a body... is the most beautiful and the most precious thing there can be.

Protarch - But this would not be at all in keeping with reason.

Socrates - So, if this is not reasonable, we would do better if we kept to this other opinion: that, as we have said many times, there is in this universe much of unlimited and a sufficient amount of limitation; and *above them a cause*, not to be disdained, which orders and balances the years, the seasons and the months and which rightly deserves to be called *wisdom* and *intellect*.

Protarch - Rightly indeed...

Socrates - Therefore, Protarch, do not think that this subject was addressed without reason, as it wants to be the ally of those who, *ab antico,* declared that the intellect rules perpetually in the universe [that is to say, the Orphics and Pythagoreans. Editor's note]»[1].

If we meditate on these passages we can conclude that panentheism was undoubtedly born with Plato. The One-Good - through Being and ordering Intelligence - is immanent and at the same time transcendent, «...this fourth which is inherent in all things...».

And, according to Plato himself, this was already the vision of the Orphics and the Pythagoreans.

Therefore we have: an ordering supreme Intelligence which places a limit (order) in the unlimited (indefinite). This *noûs*-Intelligence is therefore beyond the limit, the unlimited and the combination, that is to say the product of these two. And while in the sensible dimension the ordering Intelligence is the universal Soul, in the intelligible one it is the Good.

On the other hand, how could the supreme Intelligence create a *cosmos* (limit) out of the unlimited if it itself represented a *cháos* or limit itself? Obviously, in order to draw from it number and quality, it must have a different nature from that of *cháos*-unlimited. Now, limit-unlimited represents one of the two poles, while the other is represented by Intelligence. Thus, at the intelligible level, we have the One-Dyad. As for the One, as we said before, it does not exhaust itself in the Dyad, because «in power and in dignity is superior» to it (unlimited), just as is superior even to the world of Ideas (order-limit), i.e. to Being or germinal body, which is determined archetypal, qualified, limited, fixed and definite (known in *Vedānta* as *Brahman saguṇa*).

---

[1] Plato, *Philebus*, XIV, 27; XV, 28 XVI, 29; XVI, 30. [Italics ours]. Op. cit.

This implies that Plato was aware of the concept of the metaphysical One and of the Infinite as expressions of absolute Good. The interpretation that the Neoplatonist Plotinus gives of it corresponds to that. Even Christianity will subsequently graft itself onto this Platonic tradition in order to conceive the infinite God.

We can say, therefore, that manifestation for Plato is a limit-unlimited combination - he affirms so himself - but the One-Good is infinite, impersonal and absolute. He received the idea of combination from the Pythagorean Tradition, which recognized the existence of the even and the odd, that is the limited and the unlimited. The limit expresses perfection, the good, the determined real; the unlimited expresses the imperfect and the "evil"; from this pair (*péras-ápeiron*) comes Harmony, which the Pythagorean Philolaus defines as «the unification of the multiple and the agreement of dissentients».

One should be careful not to consider the few propositions enounced here as ingenuous and simplistic theories (as we cannot, in fact, offer here the Pythagorean Teaching).

Let us apply, as an example, these principles to the atom of physics and draw the appropriate conclusions.

An atom is made of limit-unlimited, of even-odd, of number and quality. From the appropriate *proportion* of number and quality the physical atom is born.

An atom is the product of qualified and numerically well defined particles; an atom of hydrogen, for example, differs from an atom of helium by virtue of its electronic *number*: proton 1, electron 1, while helium has proton 2 and electron 2. As atoms are neutral it follows that, in order for them to remain stable, the negative charge of the electrons must be equal to the positive charge of the nucleus. The plus-minus must balance out, just as *unlimited energy* ("field", in terms of physics) must balance out with the *limited* atom (mass).

Going into the realm of self-aware beings, we must recognize the fact that spirit and matter must balance out in order to create a human *cosmos*. Passion, self-assertion, envy, thirst for possessions are unbalanced psychological conditions which obviously lead to disequilibrium, disagreement, illness, "evil", while the pursuit of *virtue*, in the Platonic sense, means making oneself whole, it means manifesting that harmony which is the effect of a proper accord of spirit-matter, of *psyché-sôma*, of *logos*-sentiment, etc.

From a different perspectives the Platonic and Pythagorean Harmony is the right *accord* of microcosm and macrocosm, of the human being and its archetypal ideal, and even human institutions themselves must follow this rule of Accord. Wherever *logos* (positive) and material substance (negative) are out of balance there is "evil", there is disequilibrium, discord, impoverished consciousness.

Platonic *virtue* coincides with the purification of the Soul, a virtue which is philosophical and not sentimental or socially customary. The philosophical ethics is not social morality as imposed by custom and by individual sentimentality. And for Plato, the highest virtue man can pursue is a thirst for the liberating Knowledge-wisdom.

If we read that the One-Good is upright, virtuous, etc., these are not mere accidents or humanized attributes, but they mean that the One-Good has in itself perfection, wholeness or fullness, although these terms are misleading as well.

The virtues that Plato attributes to Being are ontological virtues, they are not of the sensible level or of "shadows". God is neither good nor bad, because He is beyond all possible polarity. God is impersonal, just as fire is impersonal at another level; fire can burn a building, or it can cook the food with which men nourish themselves. Atomic energy is not in itself good or bad, it *is*, and that is all; the direction we decide to apply to it, determines the destruction or to the progress of the planet.

In the infinite and finite, impersonal God-absolute, Being and becoming (world) are reconciled, and in order to comprehend the absolute-One, man wants to approach it not with the empirical mind but with the noetic one.

Turning our attention to the East, we must recognize that above all there, a deeply metaphysical vision has been professed and expounded (see Śaṅkara's *Advaita Vedānta*). The teaching, therefore centers on the metaphysical One which corresponds to the Infinite (not to the indefinite), to the non-determined and the non-qualified. These terms must, in this instance, be given the meaning that the Infinite as such is incommensurable, is cause and principle of itself; therefore, it is self-generated; and thus, it cannot be determined or qualified.

A determination is already a limitation, a circumference, a demarcation, a definition, a restriction: these terms are, on the other hand, properly applied to Being which, although finite, expresses indefinite living modalities.

Thus Śaṅkara speaks of *Brahman nirguṇa* (non-qualified and unconditioned) and of *Brahman saguṇa* (qualified and determined). In Platonic terms these are the One-Good and the Being-world of Ideas.

«And just as in the sensible world light and sight resemble the sun, yet it is not right to take them for the sun, likewise in the intelligible world it is right to hold that knowledge and truth are both similar to the Good, yet it is not right to hold that either of them *is* the Good, whose nature must, rather, be considered as far more precious»[1].

---

[1] Plato, *Politéia*, VI, 509. Op. cit.

It is worthwhile repeating and keeping in mind that the Platonic One is cause (αἰτία) of all things (τοῦ παντός ἀρχή), and therefore of the primordial polarity itself, because It is other, different (ἄλλο) and superior in "dignity and power".

The sensible-visible (ὁρατός) depends on the intelligible (νοητός) and it on the supreme *arché* (ἀρχή). So, the all is subordinated to the Summum Bonum (τὸ ἀγαθόν), to the exclusion of any factor of reciprocity. This implies that in Plato there is no trace whatever of pantheism.

PLATONIC DUALISM?

As we have noted earlier, Plato reconciled two radically opposite tendencies, that of Heraclitus and that of Parmenides. This implies that Plato recognized two states of the absolute, metaphysical Being, or Supreme Good: the sensible and the intelligible, at their respective levels. But are these two planes so separate, contraposed and distinct as to create an absolute duality?

According to some interpretations, including that of Aristotle - and many interpreters of Plato have sided with him - Plato appears to have established an irreducible duality in the dimension of Being, for which there is no connection between the two spheres. However, if rather than following one's own subjective representation of Plato's thought, one studies the Platonic texts in the light of what Plato himself states, it can be comprehended how far He was from postulating a duality or any form of absolute division of planes and of principles.

At the level of the Principles, Plato proposes three factors, which are: the Good, that towers over the world of Ideas, the universal Soul and the entities on the sensible plane. Now, the Soul, or universal Intelligence, assimilated to the Demiurge, acts exactly as the intermediary between the Good-Being on its plane and the entities on the plane of the sensible. After all, it is the synthetic tripartition expressed by all the Traditions. The universal Soul is the reflection of the absolute Good, and the microcosmic Soul is, in its turn, a reflection or ray of the universal one. All of it being a "procession" - so the Neo-platonic Plotinus was later to express himself - of the One-Good.

Hence one can deduce that there is a strict correlation among the various existential principles; or, putting it another way, the Entity par excellence irradiates its vital Principle in expressive degrees of being. We can say that, like the sun, the Supreme Good irradiates its influx throughout the totality of its own consisting. It is immanent and at the same time transcends the sensible and the very intelligible, as Plato makes us comprehend through several passages and especially in the *Politéia*: the nature of the Good, we have seen, «is to be placed even higher» than the universal Intelligence and indeed higher than the world of Ideas.

Besides, Plato mentions a "matter" (not to be confused with what we nowadays designate by the same name) as substratum and receptacle out of which all things, and therefore the planes of existence, arise and to which they return.

Here is how he expresses himself in this regard:

«The same talk must be repeated also about that nature which gathers in itself all the bodies: one must define it as being always the same, because it never loses its own power. It does, in fact, always gather within itself all things, and never in any way or in any case takes a form resembling any of the things that enter into it; for its nature is there like a molding wax for all things, which is moved and configured by the objects that enter into it; and *because of them it assumes now the appearance of the one, now of the other* (this "matter" or χώρα, *chóra,* corresponds to the *prakṛti* of *Vedānta* and constitutes the "fabric" with which phenomenal chiaroscuros are woven; the body-forms that are shaped by it appear and disappear because they are *ap-*

pearances, they are "conformed movement", *māyā*; while it does, like pliable wax, remains).

Now, that which enters it and that which emerges from it are a mere *imitation* of the things that always are (the Ideas), the former bearing the impression of the latter; somewhat difficult to explain yet marvellous.

For the time being, therefore, there are three types to be recognized: that which is generated, that in which things are generated, and that in imitation of which arises that which is generated. And, therefore, it is appropriate to compare the receptacle as well must be likened to the mother (the universal virgin Mary, or *Binah*, in sephirotic terms[1]); the model to the Father (*Chokmah* in sephirotic terms and *Puruṣa* in terms of *Vedānta*); and the intermediate nature, to their offspring... However, this mother and receptrix of all that is generated on the visible and sensible plane must not be called either *earth or air or fire or water or any other thing* that is born of these or from which these are born; but, by calling it an invisible and formless species capable of receiving all, participating of the intelligible, we are not speaking the false»[2].

The Ideas are archetypes that come into manifestation through this intelligible χώρα (unlimited Dyad; large-small) under the influence of the One-Good. This homogeneous, unitary and intelligible substratum-essence, by spreading and irradiating as far as the limits imposed upon it by the One-Good, slows down and loses its plasticity as far as becoming resistant, heavy, and difficult to order and geometrize.

---

[1] For the Kabbalah cosmogony *cf.* Raphael, *Pathway of Fire - Initiation to the Kabbalah*, S. Weiser, USA 1993.

[2] Plato, *Timaeus*, 50. Op. cit. [Parenthesis and italics ours].

On the plane of the Ideas, essence is elementary, pure, ductile, responsive and light, so that it forms perfect models, while the copies which emerge from the sensible and heavy χώρα are simple approximations. As the Ideas are ordered hierarchically and held stable by the influence of the One-Good, so are the copies ordered hierarchically by the governing, demiurgic Intelligence, reflection of the pure, absolute Intelligible Good.

The process is repeated with the Soul-Intelligence of the microcosmic individual; his bodily χώρα, all the heavier, responds the less to the ideation of the soul, so that it faces an almost irreducible material substance.

In terms of *Vedānta* the world of archetypes-Ideas represents the causal-germinal body of the entire manifestation: in it - as Entity-principle - are all determinations or seeds or ideas in their subtle state. And as in any seed whatever there is neither separation of parts nor confusion, insofar as it is a unity, so this ideal body-principle is one and manifold at the same time. As a unity it represents Being which, together with the Dyad, participates of the reality of the One-Good. If the Dyad or the Other is a reflection, a polarity or a projection of the One-Good, and all the manifest data, to whatever dimension or plane they belong, are the product of the Idea-Dyad interrelation, then only the One-Good is truly real, as all the rest is a caused or a manifested. An object, a body-volume, a solid is nothing but χώρα under geometrical form; and as χώρα is constantly in motion, the bodies belonging to the sensible plane appear, or conform according to a model, then vanish overpowered by the movement of becoming (*māyā*).

We can better specify that the intelligible χώρα, insofar as it is universal polar principle, is pure power (*śakti* for *Vedānta*) wherein all is indefinite and undetermined; it constitutes the passive complementary support of every manifestation; its correlated polarity is the *eidos*-Idea (εἶδος); thus, εἶδος and χώρα can, from this viewpoint, represent the universal polarity of essence and matter-substance, form and matter, quality and number. In terms of Scholastic philosophy χώρα is equivalent to *materia prima* (referring to the intelligible, as universal substance) and *materia secunda* (referring to the particular and sensible, which represents the support-base of the material bodies). The *materia secunda*, or sensible χώρα, participates in the *materia prima*; therefore it is a participated matter-*hyle* (ὕλη).

We say "intelligible" χώρα only for denomination and to distinguish it from the sensible one, seeing that, insofar as it is the universal substratum, it is not intelligible because there is nothing yet to be known in it; only when it is united with the Idea does it go from potential to actual, with an intelligible "datum" to be known. Knowledge is quality and not quantity and it belongs to εἶδος. This is why matter is said to be non-being, though it participates in Being.

One could say that χώρα is the mother-substance; the Idea or archetype-seed, introduced into the universal "matrix" and "nutrix", being the fruit; the One-Good, although transcendent, is the sun which gives life to and matures the Idea. The Idea in turn expresses measure, it is in fact the "measure of all things" (contrary to the opinion of Protagoras who maintained that the man-individual is the "measure of all things"). The non-measured is that which has not been determined, defined and delimited yet; it corresponds to χώρα, while that which has limit and measure corresponds to the Idea. In the concept of measure the idea of *order* is implicit; thus χώρα is ordered according to number-measure with the specific quality of the Idea.

The Book of Genesis says that upon "the Waters of the abyss", or upon the "primordial Darkness", flashed the Ray of life-giving light, so that from *cháos* came forth *cosmos*; and

God, according to the Bible, "arranged all things according
to measure, number and weight". The same is said in the
Ṛg Veda (VIII: 18, 25): «With its Ray it has measured the
bounds of the Sky and the Earth». This measuring implies
giving a geometrical form to virtual or potential space which
thus becomes *qualified*. The Ray which takes *direction* expresses certain forms: the space enclosed in a triangle cannot
but have qualities different from that enclosed in a rectangle.
The Supreme Good, by means of the Idea, gives geometrical
form to χώρα, making it qualified and determinate. Number
and quality are always correlated; where is the former there
is space-substance, while geometrical form or the precise
directions that circumscribe χώρα produce quality.

«... this fourth (the cause of all things) which is *inherent*
and in all things, and because it gives to all living beings a
soul and the use of a body... is the most beautiful and the
most precious thing there can be»[1].

In *Vedānta* texts we read:

«... the *ātman* (Being) has four parts (*pāda*= foot) and
the parts are identical to the letters (*mātrā*= measure) and
the letters to the parts... The first *mātrā* is the gross world,
the second *mātrā* is the subtle world, the third *mātrā* is the
causal-germinal world; *Turīya*, the Fourth (corresponding to
the One-Good) is *amātra*, non-measurable and devoid of
parts»[2]. *Mātrā* signifies measure, also number, and is derived
from *mā*= measure and from *mātri* which means "mother",
who is assimilated to the divine mother or universal energy
as "principle" and "origin".

---

[1] Plato, *Philebus*, XVI, 30. Op. cit.

[2] Cfr. Gauḍapāda, *Māṇḍūkyakārikā*, Chapter 1, *Āgama prakaraṇa*. Aurea
Vidyā. New York, N.Y., 2002.

Brahmā (Plato's demiurgic Intelligence) has ordered the world according to precise measurements (*mātrā*) which correspond to the sound AUM (*Om*).

Truth is one, though its verbal expressions (and often also these coincide) may change.

If, as mentioned earlier, all things created by the sensible χώρα are born and vanish (the «inversion of universal motion» takes place, *Statesman*, 270), can it be inferred that the Ideas vanish too?

According to the Mysteric Tradition - which Plato is essentially following - as the Ideas represent the *stable* and unmoving archetypes of a manifestation, they last until the end of a cosmic cycle. This is the theory of cycles and æons, cycles of manifestation whose time, though, is not chronological, as it exists on the plane of Being as continuous present. Being *is* (world of Ideas), it does not become; but, being a *determination* of the Infinite Good, its being is limited by this determination which constitutes its very own nature; in any case, its time is of an ontological order. As far as Being is concerned we cannot speak of "sensible time"; although it has birth and dissolution it does not have a *flow*; nor has it a *prius* and a *post* to which it can be related.

As regards χώρα and the bodies emerging from it, let us read this passage by the physicist F. Capra:

«...This transformation, which took place in the so-called field theories, began with Einstein's idea of associating the gravitational field with the geometry of space, and became even more pronounced when the quantum theory and relativity theory were combined to describe the force fields of subatomic particles. In these "quantum field theories" the distinction between the particles and the space surrounding them is ever-fading and the *void is conceived as a dynamic entity of paramount importance.*

...Matter and empty space - the full and the void [Plato's limit and unlimited] - were the two fundamentally distinct concepts on which the atomism of Democritus and Newton was based. In general relativity, these two concepts can no longer be separated. Wherever there is mass, there will also be a gravitational field, and this field will manifest itself as the curvature of the space surrounding that body. We must not think, however, that the field fills space and "curves" it. The two cannot be distinguished; the field is the curved space. In general relativity, the gravitational field and the structure, or geometry, of space *are identical.* They are represented in Einstein's field equations by one and the same mathematical magnitude. In Einstein's theory, then, matter cannot be separated from its field of gravity, and the field of gravity cannot be separated from the curved space. Matter and space are thus seen to be inseparable and inter-dependent parts of a single whole.

... Since photons are also electromagnetic waves, and since these waves are variable fields, the photons must be manifestations of electromagnetic fields. Hence the concept of a "quantum field", that is, of a *field which can take the form of quanta, or particles.*

... In these "quantum field theories", the contrast of the classical theory between the solid particles and the space surrounding them is completely overcome. The quantum field is *seen as the fundamental physical entity; a continuous medium everywhere present in space. Particles are merely local condensations of the field; concentrations of energy which come and go* thereby losing their individual character and *dissolving into the field underlying them.* In the words of Albert Einstein: "We can therefore regard matter as being constituted by the regions of space in which the field is extremely intense. In this new kind of physics there is no place for both the field and the matter bcause *the field is the only reality*".

The conception of physical things and phenomena as *ephemeral manifestation of an underlying fundamental entity* is not only a background element of the field theory, but also a fundamental element of the Eastern world conception»[1].

For Plato and Śaṅkara, phenomena are simply appearances, simulacra, illusions, «they are simply local condensations of the field, concentrations of energy that come and go... and dissolve into the underlying field».

Therefore, "matter", for Plato and Śaṅkara, is not a pure non-being, it is not - writes Śaṅkara - "like the horns of the hare or the child of a barren woman", that is to say, it is not a nothing but has its own degree of reality which, however, compared with the One-Good or *Brahman*, is of aleatory, undetermined, dependent nature. The effect is less than the cause, just as the creature is less than its creator. "Matter" is not counterposed to the Idea because, as we have seen, it is just one pole in a polarity. We can say that from the One-Good emerge, as intelligible reflections or rays, the Idea and the χώρα as complementary, polar aspects.

The universe is a correlated whole and presents only degrees of manifestation, ways of being, existential kinds and varied aspects of expression.

«In this way, I observed, I can make a selection: putting on one side all those who are fans of shows and arts, as well as artisans; on the other, those we are talking about now, who alone deserve the name of philosophers.

- What are you saying? He asked.

---

[1] F. Capra, *The Tao of Physics*, p. 229 ff. Flamingo, London 1992. [Italics and brackets ours].

- Lovers of shows and choirs, I explained, take pleasure in lovely voices, colours and shapes, and everything that, based on them, art knows how to realize; but how to contemplate, or love the essence of Beauty in itself, their mind cannot conceive.

- That is exactly so, he admitted.

- Now, those who are capable of aiming directly at Beauty in itself and seeing it for what it is, would you not say that they are rare?

- Certainly!

- And he who believes in beautiful things, but not in Beauty in itself, and is not able to follow one who tries to lead him to this knowledge, would you say he is living in a dream or in reality? Consider this: is it not a way of dreaming if one, be he awake or asleep, believes two similar things to be, not just similar, but identical, one to the other which it resembles?

- Indeed, he admitted, I would say that such a man was dreaming.

- And so a man who, contrary to them, recognizes the existence of Beauty in itself and is able to see it both in its absoluteness and in the realities in which it participates, and does not mistake it for these latter ones, nor vice versa takes them for Beauty in itself, well, how would you say that this man lives, dreaming or awake?

- Awake, he exclaimed, without any doubt»[1].

For *Vedānta*, too, beings live absorbed in a dream because they take the world of names and forms for the *Brahman*-reality or, in Plato's words, for the Good itself. It is the task of *Vedānta*, as well as of Plato, to wake the sleeping consciousness to the awareness of being what one really is.

---

[1] Plato, *Politéia*, V, 476 a-b-c-d. Op. cit.

The scheme according to which Plato explains the universe, or manifestation, is evident: there is an ideal World or divine Model, there is a copy represented by the world of the senses, there is an Artificer-Intelligence which models the copy on the basis of the divine Archetype; there is an elementary "matter" from which all bodies are made; finally there is the One-Good which stands above all and is the cause of Being and of becoming, although it is Itself without cause.

Thus, the sensible plane receives its raison d'être from the Intelligible, and this is demonstrated by the fact that the sensible, as it undergoes continuous change (χώρα, as we said, causes with its movement body-volumes to be born and to perish), is self-contradicting and ever becoming other from itself; therefore, it cannot be the cause of itself, it cannot be *ipseity* (self-ness), it cannot explain itself.

Reale writes, «...With the theory of Ideas, Plato intended to say the following: the sensible can be explained only by recourse to a suprasensible dimension, the relative by the absolute, the mobile by the immobile, the perishable by the eternal; the true cause of the material is the immaterial»[1].

This vision is identical to that of *Vedānta*. Śaṅkara speaks - with reference to χώρα - of *prakṛti*, of *māyā*, of "clay" of which the vessels that have different *names* and body-*forms* (*nāma-rūpa*) are made. The various chemical components are all made of the same electronic "stuff" and what differentiates one compound from another, as we have already seen, is *number* and *quality*. The ordering Intelligence, says Plato - as indeed does Śaṅkara - forges and models the "material substance" according to *number, proportions, qualities, harmony*, and this Harmony, or the archetype of Harmony, is actually realized in the ideal World.

---

[1] G. Reale, *Storia della Filosofia Antica*, op. cit.

If, therefore, the world of "compounds" is *appearance*, is phenomenon which appears and disappears, then all that concerns this appearance does not correspond to the Real in itself, cannot give - as these two Masters of the Mysteries state - either stable knowledge, or constant beatitude or Being.

«And so, said he, what remains to be said after that?

- And what else, I said, if not what follows from it? Because the philosophers are those who are able to draw from what always and unchangeably is in the same way, while those who are unable to do so, but wander restlessly through an endless number of continuously changing objects, are not philosophers...»[1].

And if χώρα - or Aristotle's ὕλη - is indeterminate, is *cháos*, is the primordial *abyss*, is formless and insentient, then it is only an effect and not the cause of itself. We can say that the "mother" is the negative polarity which, together with the positive "father" (the *prakṛti* and *puruṣa* of *Vedānta*), is reintegrated into metaphysical Unity. In Sephirotic terms we have *Kether* which polarizes itself in *Chokmah* and in *Binah*, the positive-negative polarity (or ordering Intelligence and undifferentiated Substance), from which all manifest things proceed and to which they also return («that which enters it and that which leaves it»). In the same way particles, determined by *number*, polarize into proton-neutron and electron thus producing the physical atoms, the elementary building block, or sensible archetype, of all chemical compounds.

---

[1] Plato, *Politéia*, VI, 484. Op. cit.

«Plato considers Ideas as the only true entity, while sensible phenomenon is explained by him as being halfway between being and non-being, as if something that is entitled to going only once from being to non-being or from non-being to being, something that is just a *becoming* but never a *being*. For Plato the Idea never shows as pure in the phenomenon, but is always commingled with its opposite, only confused, fragmented into a plurality of single beings and hidden under a material sheath; the phenomenon is not a thing that is in itself and for itself; its entire being is for some other, through some other, in relation to some other, caused by some other. In one word, sensible existence is merely a shadow and a parody of true being; that which is One in the latter, in the former is manifold and divided; that which is purely for and through itself there, here is in some other and through some other; that which is being there, here is becoming...

In *Timaeus*, 48 and following, Plato makes a distinction: the prototype being which is equal to itself, the Ideas; that which is formed in accordance with their model, the sensible phenomenon; and, thirdly, that which forms the basis and, so to speak, the maternal bosom of all becoming, the common factor, which is the basis of all physical elements and of all determined matters, and which in the ceaseless flow of all these forms, in the whirling of becoming, moves through all of them as their *permanent substratum*, the This, in which the forms *become and in which they again vanish*, which they never represent in its pure form but only and always in some particular form; that which takes the imprints of all forms but because of this very reason must remain itself *without any form and determined property*. That we must presuppose such an element is demonstrated in *Timaeus* on the basis of the perpetual flow of the physical being, of the perennial transformation of the elements one into the other; this phenomenon would not be possible if the determined matters as such were something real, a This, an not instead *simple modifications* of a third common element, which is, therefore, of necessity *devoid of specificity*. (Śaṅkara maintains that "names and forms" - *nāma* and *rūpa* - are nothing but the simple *modifications* of *prakṛti-χώρα*; in other contexts he speaks of "superimpositions", of "projections" which appear and disappear).

This element is more exactly defined as invisible and formless essence, capable of assuming all forms, like space which, imperishable, offers a place to all that which becomes; like the Other, in which, in order to be, all that becomes must be; while the true entity, insofar as one in itself, cannot enter into a sphere so radically different»[1].

Before going forward, we can synthesize what we have said above in the diagram appearing on page 59.

The Idea-principle is the Idea-mother-seed-archetype of the entire manifestation. It is Being that contains in itself the indefinite existential modalities: One-many.

The Universal Idea is the Idea-prototype projected by the Demiurge on the model of the principial or causal archetype.

The Dyad, the Unlimited and the sensible χώρα are nothing but the passive, receptive or negative substance-essence-polarity itself at different grades of condensation or vibration.

---

[1] Zeller-Mondolfo, *La filosofia dei Greci nel suo sviluppo storico*, La Nuova Italia Editrice, Firenze. [Italian Edition].

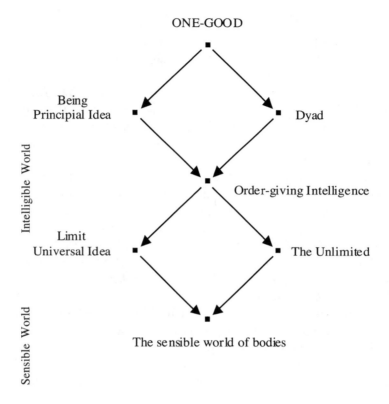

It would be opportune to "visualize" these existential spheres and the connected "descending" principles both as to keep the synthesis of the states of Being always present, and also because, futher on, we must carry out an "ascent", an upward journey, a process of integration which goes from multiplicity to Unity (according to Plato: περιαγωγή= *periagogé* or revolution, conversion).

It is well, however, to mention that all the designated terms are but symbols which enclose certain Principles or states of Being, and their unveiling can occur only by means of an actual realization in consciousness.

A last consideration: if we bear in mind that Plato was initiated also in the Great Mysteries of Egypt, then his Philosophy of the Principles becomes even clearer to us.

What does the esoteric philosophy of the Egyptian Mysteries tell us?

At the vertex of all the categories there is the non-qualified, infinite, metaphysical One, called *Tem* or *Atem*. *Tem* polarizes into *Tum* and *Nu* which represent Light and Darkness, the Positive and the Negative aspects, the Spirit and intelligible Matter or the Waters of the Abyss. *Tum, or Khnum*, and *Nu* constitute the principial polarity of all the initiatory metaphysical Traditions, although they are, obviously, known by different names.

From this metaphysical polarity, stimulated by *Tem*, emerges *Ra* (Being) which contains in itself the seeds or germs of the manifest totality.

Tum and *Nu* are also designated as Father-Mother of intelligible order, being a polar Unity and not an absolute duality.

Turning to *Nu*, *Râ* says: «You, the primordial God from whom I was born», and *Nu* responds: «*Râ*, my son, as great as your Father». In his turn, *Râ*, repeating on a lower coil of the spiral the generative act of his Father *Tem*, splits into two, *Tef-Mut* (Father-Mother), thus bringing into being the existent all. Thus, from *Râ* emerge all the universes and all the manifest entities. He represents the solar God, the builder of the worlds.

The metaphysical Trinities, being beyond comprehension for the unprepared consciousnesses, have been anthropomorphized and humanized. In fact, the Masters of the Fire of Heliopolis, of Memphis and of Thebes symbolized these metaphysical Principles with the names of Osiris and Isis (Father and Mother-bride) of whom *Horus* was born.

In Greece, Orphism speaks of a *Night* as the ungenerated and non-qualified; from Her comes forth the Uranus-Gea polarity (Sky and Earth; in other words the male-female, positive-negative, etc., polarity). From the Father-Mother polarity innumerable children are born (the World of Ideas) until we arrive at the Demiurge represented by Dionysus. He represents the first-born of the World, the God who emerged from the cosmic Egg (for *Vedānta* it is *Hiraṇyagarbha=* the Golden egg), and from which all mortals and immortals derive[1].

Furthermore, the Orphic catharsis consists in a gradual ascent from the sensible and "Titanic" world up to the world of "heavenly ether": that which is of divine in man must return to the divine.

Those who cannot raise themselves up to this state, after the death of the physical body, return to individualized and corporeal states (transmigration) experiencing corruptibility and the conflict of becoming.

The Orphic Tradition - following the one universal Doctrine - is not satisfied with the experience of the mortal and phenomenal condition, on the contrary it maintains that «every man carries within himself his own share of creative divinity and that each on e must, as a consequence, do his best to divest himself of the earthly element, and ultimately establish himself in complete possession of divinity and immortality. Orphism, like Christianity, wants the entire

---

[1] For the Orphic cosmogony cp. Raphael, *Orphism and the Initiatory Tradition*, Aurea Vidyā, New York, 2003.

man, it pulls his earthly roots and transports him into more breathable air»[1].

Plato gives new life to this same Tradition by means of cathartic "dialectics", directing it above all to persons of pure intellect.

«It is the case that these men are of no small worth, those who instituted the Mysteries: and in truth even from remotest times they [that is to say the Orphics] have covertly revealed to us that he who arrives in Hades without having initiated himself and without having purified himself, will lie in the mire; on the other hand, he who has initiated himself and who has purified himself will, when ariving there, dwell with the Gods. In fact, the interpreters of the Mysteries say that "the thyrsus-bearers are many but the Bacchuses are few indeed". And these few, I believe, are those who practiced philosophy the right way»[2].

«Socrates - You are blessed, Callicles!, for you were obviously initiated into the Greater Mysteries before the Lesser ones. And I thought that it could not be done in this way»[3].

---

[1] V. Cilento in *Mistica e Misteri nello Spirito greco*, Morcelliana. Brescia. [Italian Edition].

[2] Plato, *Phaedo*, 69 d. Op. cit.

[3] Plato, *Gorgias*, 497 c. Op. cit.

DIALECTICS AS A TECHNIQUE FOR AWAKENING

The first two degrees of knowledge, that is *eikasía* (conjecture) and *pístis* (belief), characterize individuals devoid of discrimination and intuition, essentially dominated by the senses. A predominantly mathematical mind makes use of *diánoia*; the Philosopher - in the Platonic sense - attains *nóesis*, intellection, which, once the exclusively sensory and empirical learning is abandoned, enters the metempirical world grasping the pure Ideas and their ontological links or correlations, and contemplates the supreme Idea.

The process by which the intellect grasps the links between the Ideas, comprehending their synthesis and unity, is called "Dialectics". Plato mentions an "ascending" process of dialectics and a "descending" one; the ascending process starts from the sensible, advances through the supersensible planes and culminates in the contemplation of the supreme Idea. This method is expounded in *Politéia*:

«There is therefore, I said, only the dialectical method which, going beyond the hypotheses, attains the principle in itself to fix it firmly, and withdrawing the eye of the soul little by little from, what I shall call, the barbaric slime in which it is submerged, leads him up to the high, making use of the relevant aid and teaching of the arts that had been reviewed. In order to comply with the common use, we have more than once called these arts "sciences", although they deserve a different name, more perspicuous than "opinion", yet more obscure than "science".

...And do you call dialectics also the type of reasoning that apprehends the being of each thing? And shall you not say of those who are incapable of such reasoning that, as they are unable to account for something either to themselves or to others, they lack intelligence?

- How could one deny it? he answered.

- So, as much can be said of the Good. Whoever is unable to define an idea using reason, distinguishing it from all the others, and, forcing his way, as if at war, passing through all the objections, striving to prove what such an idea actually is, not according to opinion, but to reality; whoever does not proceed in all these circumstances with an irrefutable reasoning; will you not say of him that such a man knows neither the Good in itself nor any other good; but that, even if he grasps but a shade of it, he does so through opinion and not through science; and that, as he spends this life in sleep and dreams, before ever waking up in this world, he will go to sleep forever in Hades?»[1].

The "descending" dialectical process starts from the supreme Idea and by means of *diaíresis* distinguishes between the single Ideas contained in the universal, attributing to them their proper place within a hierarchical context and grasping their operating principle. This aspect of dialectics was dealt with by Plato in *Phaedrus* and in his so-called *dialectical* dialogues (*Sophist, Statesman*, etc.).

Here is how he expounds it synthetically in *Phaedrus*:

«Phaedrus - And what is the other process you mentioned?

Socrates - To be able to distinguish the topic in its elementary concepts according to its natural connections, trying not to break any of its parts, as unskilled smiths do»[2].

---

[1] Plato, *Politéia*, VII, 533 - 534. Op. cit.

[2] Plato, *Phaedrus*, 265. Op. cit.

One can say, therefore, that dialectics represents a cognitive tool of the Philosopher who strives to ascend into the supersensible world until he captures the One-Good, and also that by which he descends *to put each thing in its proper place.*

This cognitive process is the same as that of *Vedānta*, which through *viveka* (intuitive discernment between what is and what is not Reality), attains *jñāna*, that is noetic Knowledge.

It is necessary, though, to stress a point: the term *dialectics* must be understood in its Platonic meaning, that is it must be given its original meaning. Unfortunately, many terms used by ancient Greek philosophy (such as theory, virtue, dialectics, Good, philosophy, etc.) have over time undergone such transformations and alterations that nothing is left of their original meaning. And it is important to remember that when studying Plato, not to fall in grave errors and misunderstandings.

Philosophy (which means "friend of *sophia*", that is, friend of learning-wisdom-knowledge) is the raft, the working tool, the channel through which the being is ferried from the sensible to the intelligible world. While the operative tools of the strictly speaking religious person who wants to purify and raise himself up are the cult and the rite, for the *seeker* of ultimate Truth, he who loves or thirsts to know in order *to be* the object of knowledge, the tool is philosophy. The former operates through the sphere of *feeling*, the latter through that of the *intellect*.

Being, then, philosophy a means, it tends towards a specific end. But what is this end?

«So when through dialectics, without any help from the senses contributing... one tries to penetrate the essence of what each being is in itself, not desisting until one has captured the Good in itself with the intellect, there, one has reached the aim of all the knowable»[1].

«Tell me, therefore, where the power of dialectics lies, how many forms of it are there, and by what ways it can lead to the place where, for him who attains it, there is rest from the travel and the end of the journey»[2].

For Plato and the ancient Greeks, therefore, philosophy aims at seeking the Whole, the Being, the Totality, the *arché*, the ultimate Reality on which all manifest things can depend. It is only when this has been achieved that the philosopher has reached the end of his journey and can rest.

Aristotle states in his *Metaphysics* that "knowing all things" does not mean that the philosopher knows every single empirical datum there is, but that he knows the *universal*, the supreme unity, or the constant to which the single things refer.

This is what Aristotle has to say in this regard:

«There is a science which studies being-inasmuch-as-being and the properties that inhere to it by its very nature. This science cannot be identified with any of the so-called particular sciences, since none of these others has as its universal object of investigation the being-inasmuch-as-being, but each one of them carves out for itself some part of being and studies its attributes, as is the case of the mathematical sciences. And as we are searching for the principles and the supreme causes, there is no doubt that these principles and these causes pertain to a certain reality by virtue of its very nature. If, however, those philosophers who dedicated themselves to searching for the elements of existing things

---

[1] Plato, *Politéia*, VII, 532. Op. cit.

[2] *Ibid.*

had directed their inquiry towards these principles, then the elements of which they spoke would also have been of the nature of the being-inasmuch-as-being, and not of a being-by-accident. This is why we too must succeed in comprehending the prime causes of the being-inasmuch-as-being».

«We are seeking the principles and the causes of beings, which means obviously those of beings-inasmuch-as-beings. There is, in fact, a certain cause of physical health and well-being, and there are also principles and elements and causes of mathematical entities; and, in general, every one of the discursive sciences, or partaking to a degree in discursive thinking, is interested in more or less exact causes or principles. But all of these sciences, by focusing on a particular being and a particular type, are interested only in that, but not in being in the absolute sense or inasmuch as being, nor do they offer any explanation of the essence...»[1].

And Plato maintains:

«Philosophers are those who are capable of attaining what is always unchangingly in the same... who always love a teaching capable of clarifying for them some aspect of that being which always is and cannot be touched by any kind of alteration caused by generation and corruption... And this, I said, is why the philosophers love that being in its entirety, and not just a smaller or greater part of it, or one of greater or lesser value... And therefore we must seek an intellect which, besides everything else, being naturally gifted with a sense of balance and grace, allows itself willingly to be guided to the *contemplation* of each being in itself»[2].

In conclusion, Plato's statement is completely unambiguous:

---

[1] *Metaphysics*, IV, (Γ), 1, 1003a: 20-30; VI (E), 1, 1025b: 1-10.

[2] Plato, *Politéia*, VI, 484 - 485 - 486. Op. cit.

«He who is capable of seeing the Whole is a philosopher; he who is not capable, is not»[1].

This implies that the philosopher is essentially interested in what is and does not become, in what is universally valid, in that which, among the variable of becoming, remains invariable.

Vedānta identifies the Whole with *Brahman*, Buddhism with *Tathatā*, Taoism with *Tao* and Plato with the One-Good.

«That of which the Heavens, the Earth and the Space in between, the mind with all the senses are woven, that alone is *ātman*, it is That which must be known»[2].

If, therefore, the nature of philosophy is contemplation (*theoria*) of the Whole, this contemplation cannot but transform the individual and, thus, society itself. *Theoria* is not a simple abstraction or a mere logical expression, it is a catharsis, and entails an ethical attitude. In fact, as we have seen, Plato's philosophy has a very precise aim: that of leading the "fallen" being from the sensible to the Intelligible and from there to the infinite One-Good.

Cornelia J. de Vogel writes:

«To say that for the Greeks philosophy meant rational reflection upon the Totality of things is sufficiently correct if one confines oneself to this alone. But if we wish to complete our definition we must add that, due to the elevated nature of its object, this reflection implied a precise moral attitude and a particular life style, these being considered essential both by the philosophers themselves and by their contemporaries. This, in other words, means that philosophy was never a mere intellectual exercise»[3].

---

[1] Plato, *Politéia*, VII, 537 c. Op. cit.

[2] *Muṇḍaka Upaniṣad*, II, II, 5. UTET, Torino. Italy.

[3] C. J. de Vogel, *Philosophia*, Part I, "Studies in Greek Philosophy", Assen 1970.

With regard to this point Plato in the *Politéia* states:

«This is my view: in the world of the knowable the Idea of the Good comes last, and can be seen only with great difficulty; but once it has been seen, it is recognized to be the cause of all that is right and beautiful, because within the visible sphere it generates light and the Lord of light, and within the intelligible one, because it is sovereign, it produces truth and intelligence; and that this Idea he who wishes *to act wisely either in public or in private life* must turn to»[1].

On several occasions Plato underlines the fact that knowledge of the Idea requires a "loosening of the chains", an "ascent" and a "turning around of the entire person", which means that knowledge must bring about a "conversion" (περιαγωγή or μετάνοια). Thus, Plato's philosophy and that of the Neo-Platonists must be regarded to be of realizational order, because it implies comprehending and transcending the world of "shadows" and establishing the dominion of the Constant.

F. Grégoire writes: «The reflection called "Metaphysics" is nothing but the *purest form* of that striving for unity which is the essence of philosophical thinking, it is that crucial moment in which the spirit decides, not without fear, to seek outside the world the *unifying* explanation of the "world" itself»[2].

«Because the philosophers are those who are capable of attaining that which is unchangingly the same, while those who are not capable of this, but wander restlessly amid an infinity of ever changing objects, are not philosophers...»[3].

---

[1] Plato, *Politéia*, VII, 517 c. Op. cit.

[2] François Grégoire, *I grandi problemi metafisici*, Garzanti, Milano. (Italian Edition).

[3] Plato, *Politéia*, VI, 484. Op. cit.

It is clear therefore that for Plato our quest must be directed towards what is Real-absolute, towards the Constant and towards Totality; his intent is that of finding, amid the changing and apparent indefinite data, the unvarying, the universally valid, the permanent, because what is relative or contingent - being mere effect and dependence - must necessarily have its own determining cause, which is *causa sui*, cause of itself. The method, or the technique, which permits us to distinguish between what is and what is not, is therefore *dialectics*, which is the cornerstone of the ascending process of knowledge symbolized by the "myth of the cave".

Śaṅkara who, as we have already mentioned, codified the *Advaita Vedānta*, makes use of the same technique to reach the *Brahman*-Constant.

For example, in the *Vivekacūḍāmaṇi* he begins by demonstrating that the dense physical body is not a constant, but a phenomenal compound subject to change.

«Before its appearance, it [the sensible physical body] could not have existed, nor could it ever be after its disappearance, its parabola is but a flash. Its qualities are fleeting; it is by nature subject to change, it is made of parts, it is inert and, like a jug, it is a mere sensory object. Could such a body ever be the *ātman* [the constant], the imperishable Witness of all phenomenal changes?»[1].

Dialectics, therefore, far from having the meaning attributed to it today, consists in knowing how to question and answer oneself. It is a technique that leads to proper reasoning and appropriate philosophical thinking; dialectics unveils knowledge, offers one the opportunity of passing, in

---

[1] Śaṅkara, *Vivekacūḍāmaṇi* - The Crest Jewel of Discernment, *sūtra* 155. Aurea Vidyā. New York 2005.

ascending terms, from one Idea to another, to the point of recognition and contemplation of the supreme Idea.

Dialectics inappropriately used can become a mere mental game, and when so degenerated it can lead to eristics and to sophism. The philosopher deserving of that name must raise himself up to the Whole by dialectics because, according to Plato, and also to Śaṅkara, the person who is capable of *seeing* the Whole is a philosopher, while who is not, can never be.

This dialectic-philosophical method which leads to gnosis corresponds to the Vedantic *jñāna-mārga*, the way of pure knowledge. But, for those who do not have predisposition for dialectics, Plato, being a true Master, suggested another path for the realization of the identity with the supreme Good. tThis is the way of *philosophical Eros*, which corresponds to the *parabhakti* of *Vedānta*.

If on the purely philosophical path, the way of the Knower, the operative tool is dialectics, on that of the Lover-Philosopher it is Eros.

What must be repeatedly pointed out - but the repetition is intentional - is that Plato did not devise a philosophy to gratify the empirical mind, but to realize this precise goal: to lead the restless individual up from the conflicting and perishable sensible to the supreme Intelligible, his true homeland. Plato's wish is to free the man of sorrow from the net of illusion and opinion and lead him up onto the plane of Reality and Liberty. Not only has he set out and codified the fundamental principles of the traditional Teaching, clothing it in a marvellous and impeccable conceptual garment (*Phaedrus* is considered one of greatest masterpieces of Greek literature), but he has set out and unveiled the practical, operative pathways by which to attain the supreme Reality.

Man - for Plato and Śaṅkara - is *Noûs-Ātman*; he must know how to rediscover himself as pure intelligible, abandoning the sphere of διάνοια-*manas* (inermediate empirical mind) for that of νόησις-*prājña* (intellection) by which ἡσυχία-*mauna* (peace-silence) is attained.

In Platonic philosophy, and also in that of Śaṅkara, considering the relative value attributed to it, there is no place for the world of shadows-*māyā*. The two Philosophers are interested only in the return to the One-*Brahman*. Purification by means of dialectics-*viveka* and θεορία-*samādhi* must not be confined to nullify "sin-error-ignorance" but must tend towards rediscovering and *being Brahman*-Θεῖον. The intent of the two great Masters goes beyond simple philosophical discourse, and demonstrate how the human condition is merely a moment of transition which acquires meaning only if related to the sphere of the intelligible.

Authentic liberation and true bliss consist - for them - in emerging from the dualism of the contingent, phenomenal condition and establishing oneself within the non dual One-Good.

THE SOUL ALREADY POSSESSES THE TRUTH

If we were keep our knowledge to the sensible, or only know sense objects, our knowledge would not be complete or perfect, so that we would have to be content with opinion-*dóxa* (δόξα).

Now, we have a notion of the *idea* of justice, of beauty, of unmodified reality, we have the *idea* of the perfect circle, of unity, of mathematical data, of things that is which do not belong to the phenomenal, sensible dimension.

Where from do we derive the ideas of these things that we do not see we do not feel with our senses, but that find already inside us? Plato maintains that there was a "time" when we were contemplating these ideas and that once we fell into generation we forgot them. However, they lie in the deepest recesses of our Soul; we possess them, therefore, in potentiality.

Here is a passage from *Phaedo* where this question is treated:

«And do all these examples not demonstrate that reminiscence derives from both the similar and the dissimilar?

- Yes, they do.

- But, when one remembers something on account of other things that resemble it, does not one feel compelled to ask oneself whether that given object, as far as its resemblance to the thing remembered, be in some way lacking?

- By necessity, he said.

- Consider, therefore, said Socrates, whether it be so. Do we say that an equal exists? I do not mean equal as wood is to wood, or stone to stone, or anything of that kind, but rather an equal which is beyond all these equal things and which is something different: the *equal in itself*. Well, can we say it exists or not?

- Of course we can say it exists, by Zeus! It does exist, said Simmias.

- And do we perhaps also know what it is in itself?

- Certainly, he said.

- And where from have we derived knowledge of it? Is it not perhaps the case that, if we took as our starting point the pieces of wood or stone or other equal objects, of which we were just speaking, upon seeing them to be equal, and starting from them, we think of that "equal" which is quite different from those objects? Or does it seem different to you? Now, consider it also from this point of view: do not equal pieces of stone or wood, while remaining the same, sometimes appear equal to some, yet not to some other?

- Yes, certainly.

- Well then, is it ever possible for the equal in itself to appear unequal, or for equality to appear inequality?

- No Socrates, never.

- Therefore, equal particular things and the equal in itself they are not one and the same thing.

- Indeed not, Socrates.

- Yet it is certain that, taking as your starting point these particular things that are equal, and yet different from what is equal in itself, you have been able to think of and to grasp the knowledge of that equal.

- What you say is perfectly true, he answered.

- And this, whether the equal be similar or dissimilar when compared to those particular things.

- Certainly.

- In fact, said Socrates, it makes no difference. If, when you see a thing, the sight of it makes you think of another thing be it similar or dissimilar, this is necessarily a process of reminiscence.

- Yes, indeed.

- Well then, added Socrates, with respect to equality we find in pieces of wood and other equal objects of which we were speaking a short while ago, does something similar not occur? Do they appear equal to us like the equal in itself, or are they lacking in some respect that would enable them to be such as the equal in itself? Or are they not lacking something?

- They lack a great deal, he replied.

- So we agree that when someone, on seeing something, reasons as follows: "What I am now seeing is something which wants to be like something else, that is, like one of those beings that are in themselves, but which, when compared to such a being, is clearly lacking in some respect, fails to be like it and is inferior to it"; we agree, do we not, that whoever reasons in this manner must first have seen that to which the perceived thing bears a resemblance, albeit an imperfect one?

- Necessarily.

- And so, is it not something like this that occurs in us in respect of equal things and the equal in itself?

- Yes, certainly.

- Therefore, it must be that we have seen the equal in itself before the moment in which, seeing equal things for the first time, we thought that all of them tend towards being like the equal in itself, yet were lacking in some way in comparison with it.

- It is so»[1].

---

[1] Plato, *Phaedo*, 74-75 a. Op.cit..

If, therefore, the Soul potentially possesses the truth, our task is to bring it into manisfestation. If the Soul has knowledge within itself then we must undertake to "remember" it. Plato often reaffirms the fact that "to cure the Soul" means "to purify of the Soul".

«This purification - writes Reale - is realized when the Soul, transcending the senses, takes possession of the pure world of the intelligible and of the spiritual, and joins it like that of its own genus and nature. Here *purification coincides with the process of elevation to the supreme knowledge of the intelligible.* And it is upon this power of purification attributed to *knowledge* that we must reflect in order to comprehend the originality of Platonic "mysticism": it is not an ecstatic and a-logical contemplation, but a cathartic effort of research and of progressive ascent towards Knowledge. And one can perfectly see that, for Plato, the process of rational knowledge is at the same time a process of moral conversion: in the measure in which the process of knowledge takes us from the sensible to the suprasensible, it converts us from the one world to the other, and takes us from the false to the true dimension of Being. Thus the Soul cures itself, purifies itself, converts itself and elevates itself through *knowing.* Herein lies *virtue*»[1].

In the *Bhagavadgītā* we read: «In this world nothing purifies as much as knowledge...»[2].

Here is an excerpt from *Phaedo* where this virtue (purification-knowledge) is highlighted:

«Excellent Simmias, perhaps when one is dealing with virtue this is not the proper way to carry out the exchange:

---

[1] G. Reale, *Storia della Filosofia Antica.* Op. cit.

[2] *Bhagavadgītā*, IV, 38. Edizioni Āśram Vidyā. Roma. [Italian edition].

to exchange pleasure for pleasure, pain for pain, fear for fear, larger things with smaller ones as if they were coins. Perhaps, you see, there is but one true coin, and in relation to it we must go about exchanging all other things; and it is, this coin, *the experience of a spiritual light.* And perhaps, using its value as our base, and making use of it as our medium of exchange, we can indeed buy and sell all such things as fortitude, temperance and justice; in a word, true virtue, through spiritual light; whether pleasure, fear and other affections be added to it or not.

On the other hand, when everything is detached from such light, when everything is acquired on the basis of reciprocal exchange, oh! then perhaps such virtue is a misleading perspective; servile, useless prospect that possesses no truth in itself. And it is true indeed that temperance, justice and fortitude are such a purification, and even the prudence of a spiritual light is a form of purification too. And, mind, those who have set the mystical Initiations are by no means insignificant people, but from ancient times they have chosen to express themselves in enigmas: they have said that whoever reaches Hades a profane, without having been initiated, will be submerged in the mire; on the other hand, he who has been purified and initiated, once he has arrived there he will dwell with the Gods.

Because, you see, it is a fact; and so the Initiates tell us, that the thyrsus-bearers are many but the Baccuses are few. And they, I believe, are the ones who have practised that love of wisdom in the true sense; in short, they are the philosophers»[1].

And not only in the *Phaedo,* but also in the central books of the *Politéia* this thesis is reaffirmed: that *dialectics* is conversion to Being, it is Initiation to the supreme Good.

---

[1] Plato, *Phaedo*, 69 a-d. Op.cit.

To comprehend what is "dialectics" as a cathartic means of ascent, one must first of all understand what are, according to Plato, "degrees of knowledge". These degrees, steps, or specific ways of knowledge, He expounded in the *Politéia* and in his dialectical dialogues.

* * *

So far we have expressed the Platonic doctrine of the states of Being in a simple and synthetical manner, proceeding from the One-Good as absolute, and mentioning, in descending sequence, the sphere of the universal Soul and that of the sensible being. We have also touched on the Soul which possesses within itself the knowledge and therefore the possibility to reintegrate itself into the Principle or Idea.

Now we shall speak of "ascent", "return", "ascesis", because Plato's is no vain show of mental or conceptual virtuosity, but a philosophy of *awakening* to what we really are; it is a philosophy of realization, of solution of human conflict, of return to the Bliss of the Idea.

In order to better comprehend this "ascent" or "ascesis" it is important to have a clear picture of the psycho-physical-spiritual constitution of the human being, according to Platonism.

First of all there is *Noûs*, pure Spirit which proceeds from the Supreme Good, it is the Intellect of metaphysical dimension, thus it is not thought or logical mind; then there is the Soul (*psyché*) as reflection, or moment-in-consciousness, of the universal Soul; finally there is the dense physical body, the *sôma* aspect which constrains the Soul.

Noûs, as pure Intellect, or, as it is also called, noetic Soul, is immortal, being of the same essence as the One-Good; It contemplates the eternal Truths, the world of Being. The intermediate or affective Soul is the cause of the energetic movement. Then there is the somatic Soul, seat of the sensory, instinctive, animal sphere.

The intermediate Soul can direct itself towards the sphere of appetite and animal instinct and appetites or towards the aspect of noetic Beauty which belongs to *Noûs*. Ignorance and error consist in associating the Soul with the energetic appetites (Plato's image of the black horse), completely forgetting our noetic nature; all the conflicts, sufferings, turmoils and unhappiness of the human being, all his aberrations are born of this association, and until the cause of this "fall" has been resolved no solution devised in the world of bodies can ever solve the problem. As long as passion, instinct and individualization - that is, separation from the Whole - prevail, the individual body as well as the social one will be afflicted by illness, "evil" (error), disharmony and disorder.

It is important to note that the three "Souls" are not separate or in opposition; they are elements, parts, aspects of a sole reality. We might say that they represent respectively the purely intellective, the psychological and the somatic parts of the being.

The Soul makes use of self-determination to "contradict" its own nature, thus losing sight of its noetic origin. To dwell on and associate with relative, perishable and earthly things is cause of bewilderment and oblivion of the Divine.

"Evil" is the effect of *ignorance*, it is the negative aspect of living, while the positive aspect finds its consummation in the aspiration towards existential unity-harmony, towards *Noûs* and, finally, towards the supreme Good.

"Evil" is the outcome of straying far from the Intelligible; when one falls into the abyss of bodily materiality, evil triumphs. To stray far from the essence of one's own nature means alienation; man, according to Plato, is an alienated, and will remain such if he continues to look for harmony and accord in this world of duality of the sensible (the cave).

How can one get out of this alienation? How can one free oneself from the impulses of the body and of the psychic passions and restore the Soul its wings which are capable of leading to the Divine?

Plato indicates three main pathways: the way of Knowledge, the way of Eros-Love and that of Action-acting (the *jñāna-mārga*, *parabhakti-mārga* and *karma-mārga* of *Vedānta*).

Let us now compare the psycho-physical-spiritual makeup of man according to Platonism and to *Vedānta*:

Noûs	*Ātman*
Psyché	*Jīvātman*
Sôma	*Sthūla śarīra*

Ātman is a ray of *Brahman* (One-Good), *jīvātman* is a ray of *ātman* and *sthūla śarīra* is, in its turn, a reflection of *jīvātman*.

Jīvātman, depending on the direction it desires to take, may look downwards or upwards or else assume a position of vital harmony, of consciousness balance. *Jīvātman-psyché* is the intermediary between spirit and "matter".

Again, let us bear in mind that for Plato, as for Śaṅkara, the body is just a vehicle-tool of the Soul[1].

---

[1] Cp. Plato, *Alcibiades I*, 129 - 133 Op. cit.

PLATONIC ASCENT

- *Cathartic Knowledge*
- *The ascension of philosophical Eros*

Cathartic Knowledge

Plato considers knowledge as correlated with Being because there cannot be cognition of what is not; true knowledge is knowledge of reality, and supreme knowledge coincides with absolute Good. But between pure knowledge and simple ignorance there is an intermediate zone which, although not Being, is not absolute non-being either; it is something which can participate in one and the other. Thus, there is a type of relative learning which has the name of "opinion-*dóxa*" (δόξα).

«Now, does he who knows know something, or does he know nothing?

- I can only reply, he said, that he must know something.
- And is that something that is, or something that is not?
- Something that is; how could one ever know something that is not?
- Can we therefore take this for certain, whatever the point of view from which we consider it: that which absolutely is, is absolutely knowable, but that which is not, is not knowable at all?
- Most certainly.
- All right. But then, if there be something made in such a way as to be and not to be, will it not be half way between pure being and absolute non-being?
- In between, certainly.
- Therefore, if what is can be known and what is not must by necessity remain unknown, for that which is in

between must we not seek something that is also between ignorance and knowledge, granted of course that something of the kind exists?
- Without doubt.
- Now, can we say that opinion is something?
- Why not?
- And is it a faculty different from knowledge or is it identical to it?
- Different.
- Therefore opinion has for its object one thing, knowledge another, each according to its own possibilities.
- That is so»[1].

From what we just read we can recognize two forms of learning: *dóxa* and *epistéme*, the former pertaining to the sensible world, the latter to the world of the intelligible. *Dóxa* is anyhow a degree of cognitive perception, but it does not possess within itself the certainty of truth: this is how Plato expresses himself in this regard in his *Meno*:

«But, Socrates, with this reservation: that he who has knowledge-science will always hit the truth, while he who has only opinion, however correct, will always be in doubt»[2].

Unless correct opinion is not linked to a causal reasoning, that it is not placed upon the plane of cause-Ideas; however, if opinion arrives at this it is no longer opinion because it has given way to *epistéme*.

In the same passage, Plato continues as follows :

«As also these [correct opinions] are, as long as they remain firm, quite a good thing and perform everything well. On the other hand, they do not remain firm for long, but desert

---

[1] Plato, *Politéia*, V, 476-477. Op. cit.

[2] Plato, *Meno*, 97. Op. cit.

the human soul, and so they do not have great merit, until such time as somebody connects them to a causal reasoning. And this, Meno, is *remembrance*, as we agreed before. But once they are connected, they become first scientific cognitions and then stable cognitions. And this is why science is more precious than correct opinion, from which it can be distinguished because it forms a concatenation»[1].

But Plato goes even more deeply into demonstrating the possible aspects of learning, emphasizing several types of cognitive perception. Thus he divides opinion-*doxa* (δόξα) into simple *conjecture* or *imagination-eikasía* (εἰκασία) and *belief-faith-pístis* (πίστις); and science-knowledge he divides into *median* or *reasoned knowledge-diánoia* (διάνοια) and pure *intellection-nóesis* (νόησις). These types of learning correspond to various degrees of truth. *Eikasía* and *pístis* refer to the sensible world and correspond, respectively, to the sensorial perception of the "shadows" and to the sense objects themselves which, in turn, are not real in themselves, but copies of the Idea. *Diánoia* and *nóesis*, on the other hand, refer to two degrees of the intelligible sphere. The former is knowledge of mathematical and geometrical aspects, so there is in it still something of visible, of self-representational, of operating on the basis of hypotheses; *nóesis* is immediate, direct, and pure grasping of the Ideas and of the absolute principle which is the supreme Good; it is knowledge by identity: the essence knows the essence, the Idea knows the Idea, since, as Plato says, the entity, at certain levels is itself an Idea.

In fact he states:

«... opinion is concerned with becoming, intelligence with Being and, Being is to becoming as intelligence is to

---

[1] *Ibid.*, 98.

opinion; and intelligence is to opinion as knowledge-science is to belief-faith and reasoned knowledge to imagination-conjecture...»[1].

And for what regards median or reasoned knowledge, that which is concerned with mathematical and geometrical hypotheses, this is what Plato has to say:

«...But the other disciplines which, as we were saying, draw something from Being: geometry, that is, and similar sciences, we can see that, as far as Being is concerned, they create nothing but dreams, for they cannot see it with their eyes open as long as they abide by hypotheses which they dare not question, seeing that they are unable to account for them. And in fact, he who sets as principle that which he does not know, and with what he does not know weaves conclusions and intermediate propositions, what way has he left for himself for such a sequence of deductions, as much as they may agree with themselves, to become science-knowledge?

- He has none, he answered»[2].

When, for example, we see a mirage in the desert or, on account of refraction, two moons instead of one, or the sun reflected in water, etc., we perceive nothing but "shadows", simulacra of empirical objects; when we look at empirical objects which come within the ken of our five senses, we perceive but "mental representations", not the things in themselves or the *ipseity* of these objects; we can say that we have a subjective "belief" of things, but a belief or mental representation is not knowledge.

---

[1] Plato, *Politéia*, VII, 534. Op. cit.

[2] *Ibid.*, 533. Op. cit.

As we begin to work upon the intuitive plane formulating hypotheses, deductions, analyses, etc., we can recognize that we are moving onto a more solid level of knowledge, although we may still have a mix of sensible and intelligible. When we know directly and not by means of imagination, hypothesis or sensorial intuition, then we have apprehension of a thing not as it "appears" to our senses, but as it is essentially and truly.

These levels of knowledge and the degrees of objective reality were described by Plato in his celebrated "myth of the cave". In it, he chose to summarize all his doctrine, from a metaphysical, epistemological and ethical point of view, as well as that of mystical ascent. This is how Plato paints this marvellous picture, which, by itself, can stimulate our consciousness into absolute Reality. In fact the "myth" does not make use of philosophical reflection but of the creative visualization of a condition or state of consciousness.

The "myth" utilizes imaginative representation which, disengaged from analytical thinking, reflects a metaphysical reality.

Through a "myth", then, we can grasp an "existential state" in order to *be*. Therefore this "myth" should be meditated upon, contemplated, assimilated and experienced.

«And now, I continued, imagine our own nature from the point of view of education and ignorance, as if resembling a scene more or less like this.

Imagine that there are men living underground in a kind of cavern, whose entrance, opening towards the light, is as wide as the mouth of the cave itself, and that these men have been here since infancy with chains on their feet and around their necks; so that they are unable to move, nor to look anywhere except straight ahead, since their shackles prevent them from turning their heads. Behind them shines the light of a fire burning on a height at some distance.

On the slope between the fire and the prisoners is a path, and imagine that along this path runs a little wall similar to the kind of fence puppeteers place between themselves and their audience on top of which they have their puppets perform.

- I have the picture, he said.

- And now just imagine that people are going along this wall carrying both utensils of every sort, which will appear above the top, and shapes of men and animals in stone as well as wood, of all manner of forms and styles; and that among this crowd of carriers, as it generally occurs, some of them talk among themselves while others remain silent.

- What a strange picture and what a strange kind of prisoners, he said.

- Yet very much like us, I said. Since first of all, do you think they have ever seen anything of themselves or of those next to them except for the shadows the fire projected onto the wall of the cavern before them?

- In fact, he said, how could they see anything else having been obliged to hold their heads still for their entire lives?

- And about the objects being carried? Would we not say the same thing?

- Indeed!

- And if they could talk to each other do you not think they would consider the shadows of the objects as reality?

- Necessarily.

- And if this prison produced an echo from its back wall, what do you think would happen? When one of the passers-by spoke, do you think that the prisoners would believe that who speaks is somebody else, and not the passing shadow?

- For Zeus, I would not think otherwise in their place, he answered.

- So that surely, I emphasized, the prisoners would believe that the shadows of these objects were the only existing reality.

- Of absolute necessity.

- Then, I said, if they were freed of their chains and cured of their foolishness, think of what should naturally occur to them. When someone were suddenly obliged to get up and turn his neck and walk and look at the light, and in doing all of these things he suffered, and due to the glare he were not able to contemplate directly the objects, of which he previously saw only the shadows; what do you think his answer would be to someone who told him that what he saw before were simply vane things, while now, being closer to reality and having his gaze turned towards what is more akin to being, he sees better; and, pointing to each of the objects passing before him, were to ask him what it was, and obliged him to answer? Do you not think that he would remain perplexed and think that the things he had seen up to then were more real that what he is now shown?

- Much truer, replied he.

- So, if he obliged him to look at the light in itself, his eyes would suffer, he would shun it and, turning back to look again at the things he is able to contemplate, would he not consider in reality these things to be clearer than those being shown to him now?

- That is so, he answered.

- And then, I continued, if one tore him away from that place and forced him up the steep and difficult path, without leaving him before he was lead up and into the sun light, do you not think that he would suffer most terribly and would complain at having been dragged up to this height, and, having come before the light, his eyes dazzled by its splendor, would he not be incapable even of distinguishing some of those objects which are now said to be real?

- He would certainly be unable to see, he said, at least in the beginning.

- Because, I believe, he would have to get used to the light if he wanted to see the objects that stood high up. Initially he would be able to observe the shadows very easily, and then in the water the reflections of men and of the other things, then the objects themselves and, finally, raising his eyes up to the light of the stars and the moon, he would contemplate the celestial bodies and the sky itself at night more easily than the sun and the splendor of sunlight during the day.

- Certainly.

- Finally, I think, he would be ready to look at the sun, and not at its image as reflected in the water or maybe in some other medium, but at the sun itself in its proper place and to contemplate it as it is.

- Necessarily, he said.

- And after that, by reasoning, he would conclude that it is the very sun that brings us the seasons and the years and governs all that exists in the visible world, being in a certain sense the author of all the things which he and his companions used to see before.

- It is clear, he said, that this is the conclusion at which he would arrive.

- And what then? Recalling his former dwelling-place, his science of the time and his fellow prisoners, do you not think that he would consider himself happy of the change and feel compassion for them?

- Certainly.

- And as regards the honors and the praises, assuming that they would give them to one another, and the rewards for those who saw most clearly the things going before them, and remembered most accurately what passed first, what later, and what together, and were therefore most able to guess what should come first, do you think that he could be envious or jealous of those considered honorable or powerful among them; or would he not rather find himself in Achilles' condition according to Homer, and would he not sooner prefer to serve another poor peasant for a wage and put up with whatever came rather than return to those old opinions and live in that way?

- In my view he would put up with anything rather than go back to living in that fashion.

- And, I added, consider also this: if this man were to return to where he had been and take up his former place, coming suddenly from the sunlight, would his eyes not be clouded over by darkness?

- Of course! he replied.

- And if then in presenting his opinions about the shadows he got into discussing with those still in chains, while his eyes were still blinded and unused to the darkness - and, to be sure, the time to re-adjust could not be brief - would he not be laughed at, and would it not be said of him that in going up there his eyes had been damaged, and that it was not worth the trouble even to attempt to climb up there? And whoever should try to free these men and lead them upward, if ever they should get their hands upon him, they would surely kill him?

- Yes indeed, he answered.

- Well my dear Glaucon, I said, this image must be applied totally to what we said before: the visible world resembles that prison and the light of that fire the power of the sun; and if you suppose that the steep upward climb and the contemplation of the things above represent the ascent of the soul to the intelligible world, you will not be mistaken about my opinion, because it is precisely this that you wish to know. God knows if I am right, but I believe that it is thus: that in the intelligible world the Idea of the Good is the highest and the most difficult one to see, but that, once it has been seen, it must be recognized as being *for everyone the cause of all things beautiful and good*, because in the visible world it has generated light and the Lord of light, and in the intelligible world, where it reigns equally, it has produced truth and intelligence; and that this is the Idea that which anyone who desires to lead a wise private and public life must know.

- I also share your view, he said, according to my judgment.

- Come then, I continued, be of my opinion in this too, and do not wonder that those who have risen to such a height do not wish to be concerned any longer with human affairs, but that, instead, they aspire without rest in their souls to live forever up there; indeed this, I believe, is perfectly natural, if in turn reality resembles the image that I have portrayed.

- Perfectly natural, he replied

- And so? I went on, do you think it strange that one, coming down from this divine contemplation to the depths of human misery, should make a fool of himself and look ridiculous beyond measure, if, while his sight is still dazzled and his eyes readjusted to the shadows surrounding him, he be obliged to contend in court or elsewhere about the shadows of lawfulness and the simulacra the shadows project, and to debate about the interpretation given of these things by those who have never seen justice in itself?

- In this too, he added, I find nothing strange»[1]

---

[1] *Ibid.*, 514-517.

«The myth of the cave - writes Reale - symbolizes the ascetic, mystical and theological aspects of Platonism very appropriately: life in the dimension of the senses and of senses is life in the cave, just as the life of the spiritual dimension is life in pure light; turning from the sensible to the intelligible is expressly represented as "liberation", as "release from shackles", as a conversion; and the supreme vision of the sun and of the light in itself is the vision of the Good and the contemplation of the divine»[1].

Plato's is a philosophy which indicates and leads to the "experience" of Being and of the One-Good. It is a philosophy of "salvation", of Liberation from the metaphysical ignorance in which the being has placed itself. From this point of view philosophical Knowledge and mystical-religious experience coincide. If the aim of religion is that of reestablishing man's union with the Divine, then the Doctrine of the Master is also religion, because its aims are the same, even if its operative media are different though not contrary to those of religion as such (cult). In the East religion, mysticism and philosophy are perfectly correlated and not easily separated. E. Fink assimilates the "myth of the cave" to the Initiation into the mysteries, saying that it is analogous «in its outline and in its development to the process of Initiation into the mysteries»[2], and we share in the view that the Doctrine of the Master, if diligently *experienced*, leads to the realization of *epoptéia,* the final "mystical" experience in the Eleusian Mysteries.

---

[1] G. Reale, *Storia della filosofia antica.* Op. cit.

[2] E. Fink, *Metaphysik der Erziehung im Weltverständnis von Platon und Aristoteles,* Frankfurt.

Vedānta too proposes three levels of learning in ascending order:

a)   Illusory reality (perception of the "shadow") or *pratibhāsika sattā*;

b)   Empirical reality proper that regards perception of forms (names and forms of becoming) or *vyāvahārika sattā*;

c)   Absolute reality or *pāramārthika sattā*. This is the constant or the metaphysical foundation of the sensible and of the intelligible. This reality unveils itself through the *jñāna*-knowledge of identity.

But beauty shone in its wholeness before our eyes, when together with the choir of the blessed... we enjoyed the spectacle of a beatific vision, and we were initiated, one may justly say, into the most blissful of all Initiations; perfect were we who celebrated that initiation into the most profound of Mysteries, free from all those evils which awaited us in time to come, rejoicing at those perfect, simple, calm, happy visions, in pure light, pure ourselves and not buried in this tomb, which we call body and which we drag along with us, imprisoned in it like oysters in their shell.

Plato, *Phaedrus*, 250

The ascension of philosophical Eros

The daemon Love was generated by *Penía* and *Póros* on Aphrodite's birthday. Love, therefore, has a double nature: on the one hand it is poor, destitute and lacking, on the other a lover of knowledge, audacious, and so it is in between ignorance and knowledge.

Here is how Plato describes Eros:

«First of all he is poor and anything but beautiful and gentle, as the majority believe. On the contrary, he is tough and thorny, barefoot and homeless, lies on the ground without a blanket, sleeps in front of doors or in the middle of the road and, because he has his mother's nature, it is always accompanied by poverty. On the other hand, due to what he has inherited from his father, he is a tempter of the beautiful and the good, he is courageous, audacious, impetuous, an extraordinary hunter, always bent on creating intrigue; he has a passion for wisdom, is full of resources, spends his lifetime pursuing knowledge, is a marvellous enchanter, a sophist. By his nature he is neither mortal nor immortal, but, in the same day, he may flourish and live if his expedients prove successful, or he may die for a time, but then he comes back to life, due to his father's nature... Besides he stands midway between wisdom and ignorance»[1].

---

[1] Plato, *Symposium*, 251. Op. cit.

Penía, from the verb *pénomai* (πένομαι= to work, to labour, to be needy, to take trouble), means someone who is lacking in something, who is full of worry and of restlessness from which he seeks to free himself. It is the want that urges one to become aware that he has to fill a gap.

Póros is, instead, the expression of one who has the faculty of knowing. The word *póros* (πόρος) is related to the verb *peráo* (περάω) which means to pass through or go beyond. *Póros* also implies a means to cross a river, a ford, a passage (latin: *vadum*); it gives the idea of being the cognitive means by which from spiritual poverty one attains the wealth of pure knowledge and being.

Eros, has thus two aspects: he is bereft of something and therefore he is reduced to poverty, but at the same time he is the one that can ferry us across from the wanting of the sensible to join the suprasensible whose nature is abundance.

Symbolically speaking, we can say that *Penía* represents the poor and needy sensible, while *Póros* the abundant and wealthy intelligible.

If philosophical Love culminates in identity with supreme Beauty, it may start out from the lowest level. Therefore, Plato describes an ascending ladder representing the initiatory stages of the Mysteries of Love.

Here is how the marvellous ascension of the dialectics of Love is described in Plato's *Symposium*:

«Up to this level in the Mysteries of Love, Socrates, perhaps you might be able to initiate yourself. But in the case of the perfect and contemplative doctrines to which, if we proceed rightly, those ones expounded so far are but preparatory ones, I do not know if you would be capable of it. I, therefore, shall expound them to you, she said, and will not fail to do my very best. You try and follow me, if you can. Whoever wishes to proceed along the right road in this undertaking must from early youth go towards beautiful bodies and, in the beginning, if the person guiding him guides him rightly, he must love one body only and generate in it beautiful talks; then he must realize that beauty in any body whatsoever is sister to the beauty of another body; and if it is worth pursuing what is beautiful in its form, it would be very foolish not to recognize that one only and identical is the beauty in all bodies. And having understood this he must become lover of all the beautiful bodies, calming his ardour for one body only, regarding his ardour as a small thing and trivial. Next he must consider the beauty of souls as being of greater worth than that of bodies, so that, if one is beautiful in the soul, even if not that graceful, he must be content with him, love him and take care of him, and he must seek and formulate such thoughts that can improve young people, so that later he will feel obliged to consider the beauty in the institutions and in the laws, and recognize that it is all of the same kind and thus become persuaded that bodily beauty is but a small thing. And after the institutions let [his guide] lead the disciple onto a higher plane, onto the sciences, so that he may see the beauty of the sciences and, looking at the ample range of the beautiful - no longer becoming in- fatuated, like a slave, by the beauty of any single thing, of a youth or of a man, or of a sole institution, nor being an abject and mean person, like a servant, but turned to the vast sea of beauty and contemplating it - produce many beautiful and uplifting thoughts and arguments in a boundless love for knowledge, until in this having strengthened and grown, he shall rise up to the vision of the sole science, which is the science of such beauty.

And now, he continued, sharpen the sight of your mind as much as you can.

Seeing that he who has been educated so far in amorous things, contemplating beauty step by step and in the right way, once he has come to the end of the pathway of love he will suddenly witness a beauty by its nature stupendous, and precisely that beauty for which, Socrates, the previous pains were endured, that beauty which is first of all eternal, which neither becomes nor perishes, neither grows nor diminishes, and again, is not beautiful in some ways and ugly in others, nor beautiful sometimes and not so at other times, nor beautiful compared to one thing and ugly compared to another, nor beautiful here and ugly there, nor beautiful for some and ugly for others. Nor, moreover, will this beauty take in his eyes the form of a face or of a hand or of anything corporeal, nor of a discourse nor of a science nor of anything that is in another, in an animal, let us say, or in the earth or in the sky or anywhere else. This beauty will appear to him as it is in itself, always uniform to itself; and while all other beautiful things, because they only participate in it, are subject to birth and death, this beauty cannot at all become either smaller or greater nor can it suffer anything. And when someone, having loved youth in the proper way, raising himself up from the things of here below begins to contemplate that beauty, then one may say that he has almost touched the mark. This is in fact the way to proceed or be rightly guided by another along the path of love: moving from the beautiful persons of here below, ascend higher and higher, attracted by the beauty above, moving as it were along a stairway, from one beautiful body to two, from two to all beautiful bodies, and from beautiful bodies to beautiful institutions and from the institutions to the beautiful sciences, to move finally from these sciences to that science which is not science but of Beauty in fact; and having come to the end, know that which is Beauty in itself.

This, my dear Socrates, if nothing else the guest of Mantinea was saying, is the moment in life worth living for a man, when he can contemplate Beauty in itself. And this, should you ever see it, will not seem comparable either to gold or to garments or to lovely youths and young men, in whose presence you are now awe-striken; and you are ready, like many others, looking at these beloved, to stay with them for ever, if possible, forgetting even to drink or eat only to contemplate them and live with them. What must we think, then, if someone managed to see clear, pure, sincere Beauty in itself without the filling of human flesh or colors and the many other vanities of mortality, but could see that divine Beauty in itself identical and uniform? Do you think that the life of one who can see and contemplate that Beauty with the *intellect* and dwell with it should be despised? Or do you not think, said she, that only to him who sees Beauty by that through which it can be seen, it will be possible to give birth, not to images of virtue, because he is not in touch with images, but to true virtue, because is in touch with truth? And having generated true virtue, will it not be granted to him alone to become dear to the Gods and even, if ever someone were such in this world, immortal?

And here Phaedrus, and you others, is what Diotima was saying, and I was persuaded by it, and being persuaded I do my best to persuade others as well that in order to procure for human nature such a prize there is no better ally than Eros. And that is why I claim that every man has the duty to render homage to Eros, and I myself honor him and observe the special disciplines of love and I exhort others to do likewise; and now and always, as much as I can, I praise the power and the strength of Eros»[1].

---

[1] Plato, *Symposium*, 210-212. Op. cit.

Eros is therefore philosophical yearning, the love for the suprasensible capable of having the soul, fallen into the slavery of sensual desire, grow its wings once again.

It is the philosophical ferryman that can take us from the sensible to the intelligible; it is only a means that, taken by itself, is neither knowledge nor ignorance, it is not mortal but not immortal either; therefore, it is a pathway, a road to travel, but a road that can lead us to the end of the journey «...and having reached the end, might he know what is Beauty in itself».

«Tell us, therefore, what kind of strength is that of dialectics, into which genera is it divided and what are its ways. These ways, if I am not mistaken, ought to be those that lead to where, *whoever reaches it, will find rest from the way and the end of the journey*»[1].

Plato, far from proposing a philosophy for its own sake, leading to a hopeless sterility, presents a pathway or, rather, a number of pathways - in accord with the nature of the beings - leading to where the soul may rest (the *pax profunda* of the Rosicrucian) and to the end of the philosophical journey.

«But he whose Initiation is recent, he who is full of the visions experienced, as soon as he sees a divine face or a bodily form, happy imitations of true Beauty, at first he will feel a tremor and be assailed by his past bewilderments, then he will contemplate it and venerate as a divinity; and, if he did not fear being taken for a madman, he would pay sacrificial homage to the beloved youth as he would to the image of a God or to the God himself. On seeing him, almost overcome by a feverish trembling, he transmutes

---

[1] Plato, *Politéia*, 532 e. Op. cit.

countenance, becomes covered in perspiration, experiences an unusual ardour, because on receiving through the sight this outflux of beauty he would feel such a warmth whence the nature of the wings is restored, and under its effect the sheath that covered the sprouts and which, hardened by time, prevented their growth, fuses. Therefore, as the nourishment penetrates, the stem of the feathers swells up and tries to spring up from the root beneath the entire Soul, it, in fact, had been wholly winged once»[1].

And here is how the Neoplatonic Plotinus describes the ascent of the Eros:

«And how can one reach this place? He who is by nature loving can reach it, he who truly, originally and con-stitutionally has a vocation for philosophy: being a lover as he is, when he contemplates beauty he suffers the pangs of childbirth and not being satisfied with corporeal beauty, he takes flight instead, from it towards the manifold beauty of the soul: virtue, science, customs, conventional ways; and from here he will climb once again towards that which precedes it until he gets to the root of that primordial goal which is Beauty in itself; here indeed, once he arrives, he may cease his striving; before that, never.

But how will he carry out his ascent? And from where will he get the power and what doctrine will inspire and guide this Eros of his? This one: our earthly beauty which flourishes in bodies is only something that is added to the bodies themselves from without, as these corporeal forms are in bodies as if impressed upon a material; meanwhile the substratum changes and from being beautiful it becomes ugly; therefore - this doctrine concludes - bodies are beautiful only

---

[1] Plato, *Phaedrus,* 251. Op. cit.

due to *participation*. Now, what is that which makes a body beautiful? On the one hand, it is the presence of beauty, on the other it is the Soul, which has molded and infused in him a certain form. But is the soul a beautiful thing in itself? No, otherwise there would not be some souls that are wise and beautiful and others that are foolish and ugly. So, it is thanks to wisdom that beauty enters the soul. And who is it that bestows wisdom on the soul? Necessarily, the Spirit. But the Spirit - or, so, of the true Spirit - cannot be admitted that at times be Spirit and at times non-Spirit; as a consequence it is Beauty in itself.

And yet, must we stop here at the Spirit as if He were the first, or must we go beyond the Spirit? Only in our human perspective does the Spirit stand before the primordial principle and, nearly at the doorway of Good, holds in itself the message of the universe; He is, as it were, a seal of it impressed rather upon plurality, while it keeps absolutely in unity»[1].

As regards these two pathways: Knowledge and Love, it is worth reasserting a few points: Love and Knowledge are means, bridges, instruments and intermediaries to resolve duality: in the first case Lover-Beloved, in the second Knower-Known. If these are means, one must pay attention because these can be directed in a wrong way and - as we mentioned above - they can even be degraded, therefore, used wrongly. And we have proof of this when we look at the world of men where we can see operative tools degraded in various ways and from various standpoints.

Léon Robin writes:

«Love is an intermediate essence between mortal and immortal, between men and Gods and, as the Soul has lived

---

[1] Plotinus, *Enneads,* V, 9, II. Op. cit.

among the Ideas, is the Soul's constant struggle to find once again that which once it loved and which never ceases to be loveable...

Is Love not the very means by which to create a relationship between the sensible and the Intelligible, a gift that comes from the Intelligible, an effort on the part of the sensible?...

If Love is an intermediary with the help of which we can reconcile the sensible and the Intelligible, phenomenon and Idea, it is clear that the stages of this mediation will be, inversely, the mean terms of Participation... There is not therefore a complete fracture between the sensible and the Intelligible; neither is there identification of the former with the latter and I believe that it is a grave error to make of Platonic doctrine a form of idealistic monism. But between the one and the other there is a series of intermediaries, and Love seems appropriately to be a symbolic expression of this conception. Plato had the intuition of a synthetic method: for him the effort of thought must tend to reconcile the opposites; isn't perhaps the doctrine of Love, as we have seen, one of the solutions to the problem of opposites? We can say, in fact, that it is its concrete and practical solution»[1].

If Love and Knowledge are means, then we must know how to direct them towards the proper "object", otherwise we could have an error of direction which can be fatal. Let us stress the following two points:

1) The means can be degraded, used wrongly and impoverished;

2) The object towards which Love and Knowledge are directed can be wrong.

---

[1] Léon Robin, *La teoria platonica dell'amore*. Celuc, Milan 1973. [Italian Edition].

In both cases - and it even happens that the two cases
are found together - the being or the Lover and the Knower
fall into conflict and pain. If we keep these things in mind
then we can recognize the fact that Love is an operative
instrument, a bridge that unites the Lover and the Beloved.
It is a force, a powerful magnet that resolves the distance
that exists, in fact, between the Lover and the Beloved. The
Lover has had the "temerity", says Plotinus, the daring to
separate from the Beloved, to the point of even disowning
his own paternity. The individual, deprived of the prime
source of life and of existence, has experienced the "fall"
and is obviously longing for the lost union, for Beauty in
itself. Besides, having lost the only self-giving Love, the
entity has coerced itself into cravings, desires, appropria-
tion urges to quench a thirst for Love which is instead of
metaphysical order. Thus debased, fallen, the Lover has
become restless in his desperate quest for his lost Love.
But, having forgotten the true strength that unifies and fuses
and the true object of Love, he has been obliged, in order
to survive, to transform donating Love into acquisitive desire and the true object of Love into the object that lives in
the world of shadows (myth of the cave). In other words,
Love has been transformed into egotism, into centripetal,
enslaving and imprisoning force. Instead of realizing Unity
on the Intelligible plane, the fallen being-lover tries to find
it on the contingent, fleeting plane of the sensible. This
thirst-desire to take, to grasp, to acquire in order to live,
as it brings conflict and bewilderment, gradually leads the
being to seek true Love and the true object of Love, that
is the right Beloved. It is at this point that the entity may
be called a true Lover. It is at this point that he may be
initiated into the Mysteries of Love, because, according to
Diotima's words, he is convinced by now that the world of
shadows, the world of becoming cannot help to solve the

Lover-Beloved duality. The recognition of this fact leads to a reversal of values, of aims, of relationships, of objects and all this can cause further suffering and dismay. But this is only a preliminary and inevitable phase because the entity, although he may have understood, has not as yet "comprehended". With contemplation-meditation and with the help he can receive from without, he begins to discover true Love as the *medium* capable of resolving the separation that was caused due to his "temerity". Then Love is ignited and the Lover recognizes that it is a powerful, immense, beautiful fire that tends to melt down the dividing obstacle. He recognizes that Love frees the consciousness identified until then with selfish individuality (the result of separation), to fuse it with and give it back to the Beloved.

The Lover, finally, recognizes that his will and his very life are not his but a loan that he must give back to the Beloved. A spark of the universal Fire does not and cannot have a life of its own or desires of its own, because it is simply a product of the universal Fire of Being or of the supreme Good. To feel separated from the Beloved is an illusion; on the contrary, Love springs precisely in order to reunite the fugitive and reckless spark with the Beloved universal Fire. The Daemon Love represents the greatest gift given to the wandering Lover so that he can find the source of his being and consisting.

Thus, Love is thirst for unity, for integral completeness, for fullness that offers the bliss of being one with the Beloved, that Beloved which had been forgotten and abandoned.

Léon Robin, when comparing opinion with Love, writes:

«While opinion is in a certain sense a fixed intermediary, imprisoned between the extremes of ignorance, which it necessarily surpasses, and science, which it never reaches, remaining always above the former and below the latter, Love, on the contrary, is of such a nature that it really tends to unite extremes and reconcile one with the other. Besides it is what opinion is not, because it constitutes itself a method, that is, a transition in the true sense of the word, a passage, a movement towards a goal that it attains while remaining what it is. This is why Love will be appropriately called *philosophical* in the very terms used in the analysis of the V book of the *Politéia*. Opinion is quite a different thing: one could not, in fact, as we know, transform it by means of instruction without it become something else, without having science move in, which is its opposite. The synthesis of opposites that Love achieves is therefore a true synthesis»[1].

True Love, therefore, leads to one's own home; if due to an act of the will and temerity one has wandered away from one's own home, thanks to the magic of the great Daemon Love one can return to it. Love is death of oneself because it is not desire of oneself. The Lover must lose himself completely to be able to offer himself in his total nakedness. «I seek You! I love You! I am You!»: this is the cry of the Lover who finally turns his gaze, no longer towards the world of shadows and "copies", but towards the world of Beauty and of pure Ideas. To lose himself in the Beloved the Lover must comprehend the Beloved's state of being, so as to be able gradually to *vibrate* to the same note. It is a question of sensitivity to contact, of Accord, of Beauty, of being commensurate with the Beloved Good.

«Now, if Love is a means by which to return to absolute Reality, it seems that it must have the same role as a learning exercise for death: Love is a kind of death the

---

[1] *Ibid.*

grace of which the Gods concede to us during our mortal existence and in preparation for our immortality»[1].

If sensory passion - a degradation of philosophical Love - is blind and intemperate because it does not comprehend and is centripetal because it desires and rejoices in possession, philosophical Love is wisdom, is comprehension because it is directed towards the right object, towards that suprasensible world which frees the philosophical Lover from the conflicting duality of the sensible. If desire-passion is a *ignis fatuus* that burns the higher faculties of the being, Love is a living and restoring Fire that reduces to ashes the imprisoning individualized compound, which is the cause of bewilderment and of division. Love is the death of the separated and reckless ego; desire-passion represents the life of the phenomenal ego, its nourishment. Love cannot dwell in a heart that has not been purified, just as the universal Beloved cannot be found by contemplating exclusively the world of bodies, of shadows, of names, of forms, of compounds.

If Love makes us burn with longing for the Beloved, Knowledge is the *light* which illuminates the intellect in such a way as to disperse the mists of ignorance.

Love is warmth, Knowledge is light; Love is the coagulation of all the powers turned towards the principial Beloved; Knowledge is the sparking of the light which illuminates the dark chamber of consciousness. Love fuses, Knowledge loosens the knot of metaphysical ignorance. Love is a magnet, Knowledge is a beacon, a floodlight that dispels the darkness, the obscurity of non-knowing. Knowledge unveils the object of knowing and leads it into emergence from the potential state in which it is, Love makes the Lover be attracted by the Beloved; Love attracts, Knowledge reveals, discovers,

---

[1] *Ibid.*

makes all things shine. The Knower lives on meditative dialectical tension, the Lover lives on magnetic tension.

Knowledge that has lost the true object of knowing degrades itself and thus becomes acquisition of phenomenal data, it becomes quantity of opinions losing itself into the manifold and the differentiated. Degraded knowledge leads to the quantitative inflation of data, of notions to such an extent that the intellect becomes confused, darkened, doubtful and bewildered. The Knower's conflict derives from doubt itself, from the uncertainty about the Real, from the precariousness of his knowledge, from mental confusion that depresses, stuns and makes one feel unfulfilled and misunderstood. The Lover's conflict derives from the extreme restlessness of the soul as it fails to find the object of its Love. The Lover is restless to the point of frustration, the Knower is depressed because confused, because he ignores, because the light and the object of knowing escape him.

Both the Knower and the Lover search initially in the world of phenomena, of the sensible, of shadows, of the fleeting; then, tired with not finding, they direct their attention elsewhere and meet that Knowledge and that Love which are capable, the former of revealing the Known, the latter of finding the Beloved again.

If at the beginning they utilize, the former quantitative erudition about changing phenomena - which cannot bring catharsis, ascent and fullness - and the latter enslaving and misleading desire-passion, later, after their failures and their conflicts, they begin to grasp the superior and undegraded notes of true Knowledge and of resolving, noetic and unifying Love.

Let us now compare ascension by means of dialectics (myth of the cave) with ascension by means of Love (myth of Eros). Dialectics through all its various degrees raises us to the Idea of the Good; Love through all its various levels, raises us to the Idea of Beauty.

And as the ascension by means of dialectics leads to the philosophical Initiation, so ascension by means of Eros leads to the amorous Initiation. In the *Symposium* there is mention of amorous Initiation which consists in bringing the soul gradually to ἐποπτεία (*epoptéia*, the highest of the Initiations into the Mysteries).

«...the precise meaning of the poetical developments of *Phaedrus* is that, thanks to Love, which is exactly the task of the philosopher, the Soul returns towards the Ideas, and this return consists in the recognition of the substantialized Universal, in the reduction of the multiplicity of sensations to the unity of the Idea»[1].

And as Knowledge is "reminiscence" of suprasensible realities, so Love is the condition of "reminiscence" of Unity and of divine Beauty. Love and Knowledge represent the two sides of the same coin, because Plato meant noetic or intellectual Knowledge-*nóesis* (νόησις= pure intelligence and not *diánoia*, διάνοια= discursive mind) and noetic intellectual Love (*amor intellectualis*) and not sensual, emotional and sentimental love. The Lover must of necessity be a *philosopher*, if he wishes to experience "Platonic Love".

On the plane of the ephemeral or the sphere of the sensible and the phenomenal the two degraded notes contrast with each other and offend one another; on the eternal plane the two notes - having become philosophical Knowledge and Love - integrate and fuse.

The Lover, not guided by Knowledge, trivializes and mortifies Love and the Beloved; the Knower, not guided by Love that attracts towards the true object of knowledge,

---

[1] *Ibid.*

degrades Knowledge and the Known itself. We can say that a simple eruditional effort or the blinding desire-passion do not lead to Being, to the world of the Ideas. Erudition leads to self pride, Knowledge makes one "poor" because it offers the wealth of the supreme Good; desire-passion is intemperate and sells itself in order to *have*, philosophical Love offers itself in order to *Be*.

Eros and *Logos*, rather than excluding each other, are intertwined; Eros, in Plato, is the strength that gives life to dialectics itself. Eros is love of the Beautiful, and the platonic mysticism of Love is a philosophical mysticism of Beauty.

«Plato is one of the philosophers of Beauty and of the Beautiful in itself, in the broadest sense of the word»[1].

Beauty is not, according to Plato, a particular idea like so many others, but is a universal and fundamental Idea that stands above all other ideas; yet both Beauty and Love are subject to the supreme principle which is the Good. We can say that the Good reveals itself as the Idea of Beauty and Love. It follows that intelligible Love is essentially a channel in which magnetic life-giving strength and cognitive power fuse, a channel capable of revealing the beauty of Order, of *Cosmos*. We must recognize that from the entire philosophy of Plato - as we have demonstrated - the Daemon of Love and of Beauty emerges all the while.

The Idea of Beauty and of Splendour leads us to a meditation-contemplation without form (in *Vedānta* terms, meditation *arūpa*= without form). This implies that it leads us not only outside every kind of individualized state, but also outside every kind of formal state of the universal manifested. Beauty in itself is pure essence without any kind of veiling

---

[1] M. F. Sciacca, *Platone*. Marzorati. Milano.

superimposition; a "body", to whatever dimension or level it may belong, is nonetheless a veil placed over essence.

Again, on this point Léon Robin writes:

«Love as Plato conceives of it has the characteristic of being at the same time a moving principle and a principle of knowledge, of uniting within itself doing and knowing... Love is an active tending towards the Idea, it is the enthusiastic striving towards science and towards virtue. If one wishes to understand how Love can be considered identical to the teaching of virtue - says Brochard - it is sufficient to reflect on the fact that "it is not only through abstract formulae, by means of arid demonstrations and by purely discursive processes that one elevates oneself to virtue. If nothing else, dialectics must be active and lively, reasoning must be accompanied by a warmth that animates and vivifies the Soul, by a conviction that persuades, by an enthusiasm that excites, by an inspiration that illuminates".

Love is philosopher: this means that there is in Love a certain intuition of that wisdom of which it is devoid, and the desire to obtain it; but it also means that it tends essentially to realize this wisdom in a concrete manner, both in the person of the Lover whom Love has led towards the God on which it depends, and in the person of the Beloved in whom it tries to create an image of its divine model.

...The theory of Love is one of the most characteristic forms of that synthetic spirit which animates Plato's philosophy... As such, it is possible that the theory of Love may have assumed a more important role within the system than the texts authorize us to attribute to it. Plato tended, perhaps, to see in Love the universal law that animates the whole of reality, makes nature live and moves the Soul of the world, that reunites in the Intellect the Intelligible and the sensible, that produces in the ideal world the mix of

Genera and then in the end brings them all back to and, so to speak, suspends them in the Good, under the three-fold aspect of Proportion, Beauty and Truth. A ceaselessly renewed synthesis of opposites, regulated intellectually and even mathematically in view of achieving Beauty, Truth and Good, this is what Platonic Love would mean»[1].

«...Well then, if this is what you desire, I wish to melt you and remould you in a sole nature, so that from two you may become one... but he would believe that he heard precisely what he wished to hear for a long time: to feel himself united and fused with the beloved and become of two a sole being... And the reason is precisely this: that such was the origin of our nature, and that we were whole. Well then, the desire and the quest of the *whole* is given the name of Love. Therefore, as I say, once we were one, but now due to our wickedness we have been separated...»[2].

Here Plato expounds the "myth" of the divine Androgyne or Hermaphrodite, a "myth" which belongs to all the initiatory Traditions.

Once we were a *whole*, that is we had in us the double male-female polarity, then came a split; from this stems also the division of the sexes and the laboured quest for reunion or the recovery of wholeness. This whole is the state of consciousness of the origins, not so much in the historical, but in the ontological sense. So, there was a time when the being was a *totality*, an absolute being, a unity (therefore not fragmented, divided, dual), and absoluteness necessarily implies immortality. The condition of duality, on the other hand, corresponds to mortality and conflict; it belongs to anyone who does not find in himself but in other

---

[1] Léon Robin. Op. cit.

[2] Plato, *Symposium*, 192-193. Op. cit.

than himself his own existing and his own consisting. And Plato has this state - like the mysteric and initiatory Tradition - correspond to the "natural" and "primordial" state of man. Even in the Bible we find that Adam by splitting or polarizing himself in Eve, is sent away from the Tree of Life, that is, he obliterates his own immortality.

The union of male and female, of positive and negative represents the tension, the urge and the yearning for *unity*; it corresponds to the living symbol of a metaphysical reality.

According to W. Wili «the pathway of *Eros* and that of the Orphics is one and the same. It is that pathway which from the condition of *Mystes* takes to the one of *Epoptes*, he who contemplates, who has opened his eyes [the Awakened of the eastern Tradition]; it is the pathway that from the *mysteria* leads to the *anakalypteria*»[1]. And so, the "myth" explains «the phases of Initiation, the progressive unveiling of a fundamental secret»[2].

---

[1] W. Wili, *Die orphischen Mysterien und der griechische Geist*, in "Sul concetto di Filosofia in Platone" by K. Albert, Milano. [Italian Edition].

[2] E. Fink, *Metaphysik der Erziehung im Weltverständnis von Platon und Aristoteles*. Op. cit.

ŚAṄKARA

It is difficult to establish Śaṅkara's date of birth. According to the tradition he was born in the year of *Nandana*, in the lunar month of *Vaiśākha* (April-May), on the day of *sukla-pañcami*: but which year of the *Nandana*? According to some scholars Śaṅkara was born around the year 700 A.D., because in his *Brahmasūtrabhāṣya* (IV, II, 5) there is mention of the city of Pataliputra, which was destroyed by fluvial erosion around 750 A.D.

A Sanskrit manuscript gives the birth and death of Śaṅkara as: Kali 3889 and 3921 which correspond with 788 and 820 A.D. The same date, Kali 3889, is also mentioned in the *Śaṅkara-mandara-saurabha* work.

The people of Kālaṭi - a village on the banks of the Cūrṇā river in the Kêrala region where Śaṅkara was born - saw the newborn baby in the home of Śivaguru, Śaṅkara's father, and thought it was truly Śambhu (Śiva) come as an *Avatāra* (incarnation of a universal principle).

On the eleventh day after his birth, the baby was given the name of Śaṅkara, the letters of which indicate the day, the fortnight and the month of his birth.

Śivaguru chose this name for his son without any reference to its significance; but it turned out to be meaningful because Śaṅkara is held to be an *Avatāra* of Śiva.

The most relevant events of Śaṅkara's life are contained in the following Sanskrit verse: «At the age of eight he had already mastered the four *Vedas*; at twelve he was well versed in all the *Śāstras*; at sixteen he finished compiling his *bhāṣya* (his commentary to the *Brahmasūtra*) and at thirty-two he abandoned this world».

Before the *upanayanā* (investiture with the sacred cordon) could be carried out, Śivaguru died and the *upanayanā* took place instead when Śaṅkara was five. He was sent to a *gurukula* (the hermitage of a *guru*) to carry out his Vedic studies. He soon mastered the wisdom contained in the six auxiliary branches of the *Vedas* and in the other *Śāstra*. As a *brahmacārin* he lived on alms and by serving his instructor.

Having completed his tuition, Śaṅkara left the *gurukula* and went back to live with his mother Āryāmbā. When he was still very young he asked his mother's permission to leave the village and seek a *guru* (teacher) to initiate him into formal *saṁnyāsa* (the ascetic renouncer). Before leaving he provided for her maintenance and protection. He promised to return whenever his presence was required and to perform personally the last rites after her death.

After a long journey he reached the banks of the river Narmadā where he found his Master. Govinda Bhagavat-pāda, Gauḍapāda's disciple, lived in a cave surrounded by a few learned and wise men who had chosen him as their guide. Śaṅkara stood at the mouth of the cave in which Govinda sat and announced his arrival asking him to accept him as his disciple. Govinda asked him: «Who are you?». Śaṅkara's answer consisted in explaining the nature of the supreme Self in the ten verses known as the *Daśaślokī*. By applying the dialectical method and proceeding by exclusion, Śaṅkara demonstrated that, beyond transient phenomena, beyond empirical appearance or the world of names and forms, there is one Reality always equal to itself as the metaphysical foundation of being and of non-being; this Reality without a second is *our* reality.

Govinda was pleased with Śaṅkara's masterly exposition of *Advaita* (non-duality) and accepted him as a disciple. As was the custom, he was initiated into *paramahaṁsa-saṁnyāsa* and was instructed according to the *mahāvākya* (the chief sayings of the *Upaniṣad*) which teach the truth of non-duality.

Śaṅkara came not to destroy but to edify, and the philosophy he imparted, the *Advaita*, must not be viewed as being in opposition to the other schools of thought. Śaṅkara's *paramaguru*, Gauḍapāda, had already taught that there could be no antagonism between *Advaita* and the dualistic philosophies. Just as a person cannot disagree with his own limbs, so *Advaita* cannot oppose any of the other philosophical systems.

Śaṅkara, who rediscovered the spirit of unity and of totality and revealed it at a time of tumult and discord, tried to put an end to divisions and to put the parts back in their position in the context of the whole. His message consists in claiming not only the non-duality of *Brahman* (*Brahmādvaita*), but also the fundamental non-difference of the other "points of view" (*darśana*). To do this, he simply followed the teaching of the *Veda* which proclaim this supreme truth: «Reality is one», and then add that: «This Reality is given many names».

The orthodox and heterodox schools alike gained from Śaṅkara's constructive dialectics. Although their starting points of view differed, *Mīmāṁsāka* and Buddhism had become unusual fellow soldiers in defence of atheistic doctrines. Śaṅkara had to correct the one-sidedness of both doctrines: *karma* or ritual was assigned its proper place as propaedeutic to the pathway of knowledge; the noble doctrine of *ahiṁsā* (non-violence), underlined by Buddha but not unknown to the *Veda*, was included as an essential part of the Hindu philosophy of *dharma*, and Buddha himself considered as an *Avatāra* of Viṣṇu.

Like philosophy, religion too gained from Śaṅkara's teaching. He wanted to preserve the faiths and their institutions by removing the superstructures that with time had penetrated them, thus restoring them in their original genuineness and pointing them out as different modes of approaching» the Divine.

According to Śaṅkara the personal Divinity (the God person) is not the highest expression, but aspiration towards It is a necessary step in the realization of *Advaita*. If that be so, then not the name by which God is known matters, but the firm and innocent aspiration of the neophyte. In his *Hymn to Hari* Śaṅkara declares:

«Glory to Hari, who dispels the darkness of *saṁsāra* (phenomenal becoming), the sole Reality which, due to the diversity of beings, manifests itself under many names such as Brahmā, Viṣṇu, Rūdra, Agni, Sūrya, Chandra, Indra, Vāyu and Sacrifice».

The foundation of religion is the same, although its manifestations are many. Śaṅkara professed pure universalism and in his philosophy he rendered homage to Being in its various aspects.

In the light of *Advaita,* he wrote commentaries to the three fundamental texts of *Vedānta*: the *Upaniṣad*, the *Bhagavadgītā* and the *Brahmasūtra*. Besides the *bhāṣya* (commentaries) he wrote many texts concerning *Advaita* such as *Ātmabodha, Vivekacūḍāmaṇi, Upadeśasāhasrī* and *Aparokṣānubhūti*.

Śaṅkara died very young, at only thirty-two years of age, but these few years were sufficient to enounce and codify the

Advaita Vedānta, to write commentaries to the main Vedic texts, to reorganize the *Svāmi* orders, to found four *Maṭha* (centres of realization) situated at the four cardinal points of India, and kindle in the hearts of his people a love for realization through metaphysics[1].

---

[1] We are indebted to Prof. T.M.P. Mahadevan for this brief note on Śaṅkara. For further information regarding the life of Śaṅkara see *Śaṅkara and Kevalādvaita-vāda* by Prof. Mario Piantelli. Edizioni Āśram Vidyā, Rome. [Italian Edition].

PLATONISM AND VEDĀNTA

From what has been said on Plato's teaching one may draw the following concordances with Śaṅkara's *Advaita Vedānta*.

1. The two teachings postulate a Constant as *causa sui*, on which the Whole depends.

2. They give the same definition of the term "reality". Real is that which is permanent, unchangeable and *universally* valid, that which has neither origin nor end, that which is *identical* to itself.

Plato, like Śaṅkara, identifies Being, Identity and Immobility with the supreme Good; and becoming, variation and motion with the empirical sensible.

3. They formulate a hierarchy of existential planes and of ethical values that are essentially identical.

4. They conceive of conflict, pain and of the contradictions of the human condition as the effect of a fall-oblivion-*avidyā*.

5. They view the sensible world as a "shadow", a projection lacking in real depth and consistency, although they do not consider it a "nothing", a non-being in absolute terms. The sensible has no independent reality of its own; it is but an indeterminate, devoid of any positive characteristic, assuming existence only when it is animated by what Plato calls

Idea and what Śaṅkara refers to as *Īśvara* at the universal level, or *ātmā* at the individual level.

For Śaṅkara the sensible world is not a "nothing" as would be "the horns of a hare or the child of a barren woman", but it is nonetheless not an absolute, therefore, unable to offer stable Knowledge.

6. They conceive the entity, in its integrity, as made up of the sensible and the suprasensible, capable of recognizing the latter and of realizing it.

F. Grégoire writes: «Plato's is a tempered idealism which, without denying in absolute terms the existence of things, does not see in them anything but a secondary world of appearances and confusion; this imperfect world has no significance except as a function of the intelligible universe, a universe of pure Ideas, of which it constitutes but a hazy reflection. It is however possible for men to go beyond our sensible world and raise themselves up to the contemplation of these true, perfect and eternal Ideas, for which it is necessary to undertake a special spiritual activity which Plato calls "dialectics" and which consists in a sort of gradual and reasoned purging of the changeable and imprecise aspects that earthly things offer us, to arrive, by means of these, at a discovery of the Ideas which they imitate in a gross manner»[1].

These considerations can be applied wholly and without exception to the teaching of Śaṅkara[2].

7. They recognize the empirical mind possesses the faculty of expressing "opinions" and apprehending phenomena only; but they also attribute to the entity the ability

---

[1] François Gregoire, *I grandi problemi metafisici.* Op. cit.

[2] For the levels of knowledge in *Vedānta* cp. Raphael, *Tat tvam asi (That thou art),* Chapter 5. Aurea Vidya, New York, 2003.

to apprehend through pure contemplation and pure noetic, intellectual intuition.

8. Both Teachings strike an optimistic note and offer great philosophical comfort; man can raise himself up from his spiritual, psychological, and material debasement and solve all his existential problems; he can thus escape the grip of suffering and contradiction in which he lives. These are, therefore, teachings of "Salvation", of Liberation, of catharsis.

9. Plato and Śaṅkara are not so much the initiators of new religions, as their reformers; they are not so much the propagators of a new metaphysical and religious vision, as restorers of a degraded religious tradition, strayed from the metaphysical principles.

Śaṅkara and Plato stand as "rectifiers" of *Vedānta* and the *Mysteries* Visions respectively, both degraded by the hands of priests not qualified to fulfill their functions. Thus they both act within the scope of a precise renewal of the religious Tradition, reintegrating it in its original purity. Both extend the spiritual Vision beyond caste individualism, and indeed *polis*, restoring vigour to the universal vision of Being. From this stems the development of the Great Mysteries or of *paravidyā* (supreme knowledge, as distinct from *aparavidyā* or relative, second knowledge).

10. The two masters live, write and act in accordance with the Teaching they profess.

11. Plato's philosophy is not a mere personal speculation by the empirical mind, nor a dialectical virtuoso performance, but the continuation of Orphic and Pythagorean Teaching. We must remember that Plato was one of the great initiates into the Sacred Mysteries of Greece and Egypt.

Śaṅkara's *Advaita Vedānta* follows the same path, referring back to the *Veda-Upaniṣad*.

12. Plato draws from the traditional Mysteries primarily
the metaphysical content (Greater Mysteries), which is for
the few, while leaving to the many the more ritualistic and
preparatory content (Lesser Mysteries). Even at the social
level he makes a distinction between the ideal state of the
Politéia and the more "humanized" one of the *Laws*.

Similarly Śaṅkara leaves aside the Vedic ritualism of
the *Mīmāṁsā* in order to give expression to the essentially
metaphysical part *(paravidyā)* of the *Veda-Upaniṣad*.

13. In as much as it is traditional and sacred philosophy,
it is of a cathartic, realizative order; and this Plato, like
Śaṅkara, asserts unequivocally. This shows that both Plato
and Śaṅkara did not write for the sake of mere "discursive-
ness" as an end in itself, but to point out a "road", a "way"
of realization, of salvation, of liberation of the Soul from
the shackles of ignorance.

14. Leaving aside the ritual aspect, the Platonic Teaching
places the accent above all upon Knowledge as the direct
means of purification of the Soul and its elevation to the
intelligible. Speaking in terms of *Vedānta* this corresponds
to Śaṅkara's *jñāna-mārga*, or way of Knowledge.

15. Plato, like Śaṅkara, places as the principal object of
human attention the intelligible Soul, considering the world
of bodies or of the sensible, as an expression of corruption and of conflict. This implies that, like Śaṅkara, he
reverses the values of life - as it is commonly understood
- by placing Reality as such not in the world of becoming
but in that of Being, since the world of becoming is simply
one of "shadows" which appear and disappear. Thus, for
Plato, as for Śaṅkara, philosophy is an "exercise of death",

involving the solution of *avidyā*-ignorance, that is the sensible-corruptible, the shadow. Under other perspectives, one could say that for them seeking true life is a philosophical exercise in authentic living, a living that responds to the pure dimension of the Spirit.

The "flight" from the body and the world is flight indeed, but not towards annihilation and evasion, rather towards the true Homeland of Being; it is a flight from the world of shadows, from the sensorial-passional-irrational. The flight for Plato and Śaṅkara is directed at rediscovering the supreme Good or *Brahman*.

This Platonic "renunciation" is based upon a *cognitive factor*, on an act of spiritual Dignity which, once awakened, gives man the capacity to comprehend himself and recognize himself of intelligible lineage. The Platonic renunciation is not the outcome of "mortification", of emotional "repentance", of psychological complexes or such like. The "flight" of Plato, or of Śaṅkara, follows naturally from the recognition of the fact that one is of supranatural nature. Knowledge, or the "remembrance" of what one really is, causes every "grasp", "lust" or "thirst" in the corruptible world to be split, shattered and transcended. Those who clearly *comprehend*, in its nakedness, the "play" of becoming (*saṁsāra* for *Vedānta*) no longer allow themselves to be tricked.

The Platonic flight is not a running away from physical or psychological pain, nor from whatever responsibilities the individual may have, it is something more; it is the flight of the philosopher who, by means of pure contemplation, has *comprehended* the inadequacy, the ephemerality, the vanity, the inconsistency or the non-substantiality of the material sensible sphere.

We shall say more: the Philosopher's is no flight at all, for what needs he flee from if things are not? Plato's flight is thus directed towards the land of *our true fathers* (World of Ideas), because this land of the sensible plane, is merely a playground for those who are asleep.

«For this reason we too must endeavour to flee from here to up there as soon as possible. Flight means rendering ourselves similar to God (ὁμοίωσις Θεῷ) according to our own possibilities: and rendering ourselves similar to God means becoming just and holy, and wise too»[1].

But let us be clear: the Knowledge of which we speak is that indicated by Plato and Śaṅkara, that which brings about a *conversion* and makes us discover the Dignity of being divine.

16. Both Masters - as mentioned already - did not disown the religion of their forefathers, nor its rituality, but sought to purify them of the excesses into which they had fallen. The following quotation from Zeller-Mondolfo, supported by the relevant references from Plato, is emblematic:

«First of all, for what regards religion, ...for our philosopher true religion identifies with philosophy, and the truly divine identifies with the supreme objects of philosophical speculation. Philosophy is for him not only a theoretical attitude but equally a practical one, it is *love* and *life*, full *realization* of man by means of the true entity and of the truly infinite... Just as above all the Ideas, and as the cause of all being and knowing, stands the supreme Idea, so above all the Gods, and equally difficult to find and describe, stands the sole, eternal, invisible God, the creator and father of all things (see *Timaeus*, especially 28c, 29e, 34a, 41a, 92b)... Not only does he reject the anthropomorphic conception whereby the Divinity would have a body,

---

[1] Plato, *Theaetetus*, 176 b. Op. cit.

but also all the other anthropopatic tales that attribute passions, disagreements and crimes of all kinds to the Gods; he states that they are superior to pleasure and disgust (*Philebus*, 33b) and are untouched by any evil, strongly and with great moral indignation opposing the opinion whereby it is possible to placate them, or rather corrupt them, with prayers and sacrifices. He demonstrates, besides, that all is ordered and governed by divine providence and that the care of providence extends to the small as well as the great (*Timaeus*, 30b, 44c; *Sophist*, 265c and following; *Philebus*, 28 and following, *Laws*, IV, 709b; X, 899d).

...For the state and the majority of citizens he wishes, therefore, to preserve the popular faith and the traditional cult of the Gods, but the one and the other must be purified from a moral point of view, and the excesses towards which, even in those times, their representatives were inclined must be prevented; indeed in *Laws* (X, 907d) he proposes severe punishment, not only against atheism and other crimes of a religious nature, but also in the case of private cults and the abuses arising from them [hence we can deduce that he has been a "rectifier" of the Tradition].

... What gave his philosophy a warmth and a practical direction which go beyond his scientific principles, what made him feel the necessity of the closest possible adherence to the popular faith, was that moral-religious interest which he felt, as a true follower of Socrates, to be intimately linked with the scientific one... He shows us that in the enthusiastic love for Beauty, common and prior to all knowledge, lies the root of morality and philosophy, he points out to us that non-philosophical virtue is a preparatory step towards philosophical virtue, that religious faith is analogous to philosophical intelligence, an analogy which in the case of the majority of men must act as a substitute for that intelligence»[1].

This consideration of Zeller-Mondolfo's concerning Plato can also be applied to Śaṅkara who set for himself the same objective.

Examining the hierarchical structure of Being, Plato expresses it as follows:

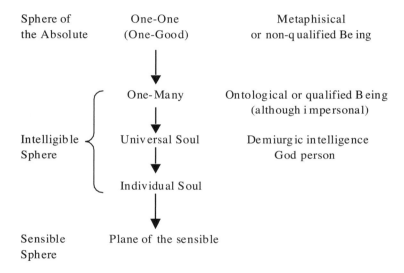

Sphere of   One-One   Metaphisical
the Absolute   (One-Good)   or non-qualified Being

                   One-Many   Ontological or qualified Being
                                          (although impersonal)

Intelligible   Universal Soul   Demiurgic intelligence
Sphere   God person

                   Individual Soul

Sensible   Plane of the sensible
Sphere

The One-One, or supreme Good, corresponds to *Turīya*, or Fourth, or *Brahman nirguṇa* (non-qualified) of *Vedānta*. It is the metaphysical Being in the strict sense of the word, or the Non-Being, because it is beyond the bounds of qualified or principial Being. Therefore Non-Being, because it can be neither the One as efficient cause of the manifested

---

[1] Zeller-Mondolfo, *La Filosofia dei Greci nel suo sviluppo storico*. Op. cit.

multiplicity, nor differentiated multiplicity, or duality. The Non-Being, or metaphysical Being, due to its particular nature, must include Being and non-being and, at the same time, It must be beyond Being and non-being. This corresponds equally to the *Ain-Soph* of the *Qabbālāh*.

Of It, all that we can really say is that "it is what it is"; that is all.

«Therefore, you may say that knowable things derive from the Good not only their knowability, but also their existence and essence, although Good is not essence but for dignity and power is even above essence»[1].

The One-Many represents the causal Body, the universal seed which contains the unlimited possibilities of Being. It is "one" because there is in it no absolute separation of the parts, therefore there is no duality; it is "many" because in Unity is contained the archetypal synthesis of all that exists upon the manifest plane. It corresponds to *Īśvara* or *Brahman saguṇa* (qualified) of *Vedānta*, to that *Brahman* that contains, in fact, all the archetypal determinations of manifestation. It must be regarded as the causal, germinal Body - mentioned above - in that in It dwell at one and the same time all the causes-categories which will develop as effects- reflections on the plane of the universal intelligible and on the plane of the individualized sensible.

The One is Being; the many, within Unity, are the figures, the various or multiple modalities or expressions of the One. Thus, our mind - let us take the example of dreaming - is capable of projecting an indefinite amount of data while still remaining one mind. This is the ontological sphere of Being, the sphere in which all things are born and to which all things return.

------

[1] Plato, *Politéia*, VI, 509. Op. cit.

«The world of Ideas is a world of impersonal beings. Even the supreme Idea, that is the Good in Plato's *Politéia* (or the One of the "unwritten doctrines"), is *theion* (Θεῖον) and not *theos* (Θεός), an *impersonal* Divinity and not a God person»[1].

As the seed of a flower, though a unity, contains in itself all the categories of its expression: the stem, the leaves, the petals, the corolla etc., so the universal Seed contains in itself all the potential determinations or expressive categories, which on the manifest plane reveal themselves in the manifold entities of every type and degree. And as the various components of the flower can cause neither absolute duality nor confusion, resting as they do upon the sole reality and upon the common basis of being, so the manifold Ideas, however different from one another, all rest upon their common basis which is the one Being. We can even say that multiplicity is the indefinite life mode of the One-All.

This Seed, the ontological basis, is brought into manifestation or given expression by the demiurgic, ordering Intelligence, which moulds the pregenetic substance-matter, or χώρα (the *prakṛti* of *Vedānta*) to produce prototypes as close as possible to the seed-Model; these prototypes are "projections", "copies", reflections of light-shadows that appear and disappear.

As one descends through the planes or life's modes of expression, the perfection of the prototypes diminishes because the *chóra*-matter becomes all the more heavy and opaque, less responsive and plastic to the archetypal Idea. As one descends from the *simple* to the *compound*, the manipulation of the substance becomes increasingly difficult, thus presenting precise limits in terms of response and perfectibility.

---

[1] G. Reale, *Storia della Filosofia Antica*. Op. cit.

The Intelligence, personified by the Demiurge - as universal Soul - is a "product" of the ideal intelligible world, wherefore it has three data before it:

- The intelligible world.
- The χώρα-matter, or formless substance.
- The contemplative action.

In Vedantic terms it corresponds to *Brahmā*, to the creator which, activated by the energy of *Śiva*, brings the Seed of *Īśvara* into manifestation or objective expression. *Brahmā*, insofar as it is the creator, or rather, the universal orderer-moulder, is often assimilated to *Hiraṇyagarbha*, the Golden Egg from which the totality of existing entities emerge.

In turn, the human Soul is a ray of light, a spark of the universal Soul, and - like the latter - it also has three data before it (plus a fourth, when it is able to perceive and contemplate it):

- The universal intelligible world, which for it represents the ideal Model, when it is able to grasp it (hence the various degrees of initiation).

- Its χώρα-substance (individualized portion of the universal substance) upon which it must exert its ordering action.

- The contemplation of the Idea.

In Vedantic terms, the microcosmic Soul corresponds to the *ātmā* which dwells upon the plane of *buddhi*, that is to say upon the plane of universal Intelligence or of pure intellect (*sattva*), and from there it casts its reflections on the concrete-sensible.

To facilitate the task for those who may not be familiar with the philosophy of Plato and of Śaṅkara, the following scheme summarizes the subject (see page 135).

«And, to this end, Plato too teaches us his three degrees: Everything - he says (and is referring to that which is first) - centers around the King of the All and the second around the Second, and the third around the Third. But he also states that the cause has a father, that cause which - as he himself says - is the Spirit; the creator, in fact, for him is the Spirit; This one - he says - creates the Soul in that cup of his. And the father of the cause - which is really the Spirit - he calls it "the Good" and "That which is beyond the Spirit and beyond Being"; and in many places he calls Being and Spirit, Idea. Therefore Plato is aware that the Spirit (Idea) is derived from the Good and that the Soul is derived from the Spirit. Thus these reasonings of ours are nothing new, nor do they date from today, but were put forward a long time ago even if not explicitly, and our present discussions are only interpretations of discussions of ancient times, which stand as guarantee that these doctrines are in fact of ancient origin, coming down to us through his writings, of Plato himself. Thus, even Parmenides, before Plato, touched on this doctrine, in that he identified Being with Spirit, and placed Being outside the realm of sensible things, "because thinking is the same as being" - he said; and he continues by saying that Being is immobile although he adds thinking to it and takes all movement from it, in order that it might continue as identical; and he resorts to the image of a spherical mass, because it embraces all things tied together and because his thought as inside and not external of it. Using the term "One" in his writings, however, he made himself vulnerable to criticism, because this "One" of his turns out in the end to be "many things";

Expression of the Being

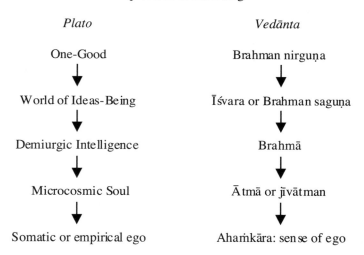

Plato	Vedānta
One-Good	Brahman nirguṇa
↓	↓
World of Ideas-Being	Īśvara or Brahman saguṇa
↓	↓
Demiurgic Intelligence	Brahmā
↓	↓
Microcosmic Soul	Ātmā or jīvātman
↓	↓
Somatic or empirical ego	Ahaṁkāra: sense of ego

Existential planes

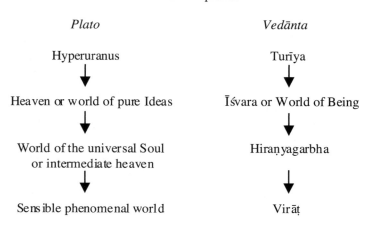

Plato	Vedānta
Hyperuranus	Turīya
↓	↓
Heaven or world of pure Ideas	Īśvara or World of Being
↓	↓
World of the universal Soul or intermediate heaven	Hiraṇyagarbha
↓	↓
Sensible phenomenal world	Virāṭ

on the other hand Plato's *Parmenides* talks with greater critical accuracy, distinguishing between the primordial One, which is more appropriately called One, the second, which he calls "One-Many", and the third, which is "One and the many". Thus, he too agrees with the doctrine of the three natures, exactly in the sense we attribute to it»[1].

We regard Plato's message, addressed to men on the sensible plane, as being the highest and the most fruitful the human mind has ever been able to conceive.

To comprehend it well, one must consider, first of all, the bases upon which He attempts to construct the mysticism of liberation of the individual in conflict. For him this event represents a categorical imperative.

The first factor upon which Plato postulates his vision of realization rests on the fact that man has fallen into a state of *oblivion* with regard to his true *origin*. Man is a Divinity that has forgotten himself; he is a stunned Daemon, a slave of the phenomenal or sensible world, because he has *forgotten* what he really is. In his totality, he is not only body, *sôma*, nor is he only mind or only Soul, he is also an Idea, a Being; rather, he is Being, because Being is one.

What we have described here is identical to the vision of *Vedānta*, to the upaniṣadic "That thou art" (*Tat tvam asi*) and to all the other eastern and western initiatory Doctrines.

The first aim, therefore, must be that of *remembering* one's origin so as to recover one's own Dignity.

If the reason of life is to *remember*, this implies that the being has within himself the solution to the problem of life. Knowledge, that is true Knowledge, is not what concerns the sense objects, which are only changeable shadows projected upon the great screen of χώρα, but that which operates di-

---

[1] Plotinus, *Enneads*, V, 1, VIII. Op. cit.

rectly in the noetic world of pure Ideas. Knowledge does not mean apprehending or acquiring something that one does not have, it does not mean "taking possession" of the truth, but an *unveiling*, a means capable of bringing Truth from virtuality to actuality. Knowing is *seeing*, and *seeing* is knowing, but knowing-seeing means *awakening* to what one really is.

Platonic *anámnesis* (remembrance) is awakening to the reality of the intelligible, and this implies a turning, a complete conversion of one's own consciousness.

Μετάνοια-περιαγωγή represents a deep re-thinking, a change in one's way of feeling and judging things, and Plato's philosophy leads inevitably to such a state of being.

«Now then, I continued, if all this is true, we must conclude as follows: education is not what certain people pretend it is. These claim, I believe, that even when in a soul there is no knowledge they can put it there, as if giving sight to blind eyes.

- That is indeed what they claim, he answered.

- While on the other hand, I said, our reasoning indicates that in the soul of each one of us there is *the faculty to apprehend* and the *organ* by which each person learns; and just as the eye is unable to turn from darkness to light only but with the entire body, so this organ of the soul must be *turned away* in its entirety from *that which constitutes becoming* until it is capable of *contemplating Being* and of contemplating it in its luminous part which is, as we affirm, the Good. Or do you not think so?

- Of course.

- Education, therefore, I said, is the art of bringing about this *revolution*, and bringing it about in the easiest and most useful manner; it is not the art of implanting in man the faculty of sight, but of procuring to him who *already possess that faculty*, but are turned the wrong way and do not look where he should, the possibility of achieving this *conversion*»[1].

In the sensible world, knowledge is mere opinion (δόξα) because it does not give absolute certainty; things-events in the realm of the sensible undergo continuous change and mutation, for which reason they cannot possibly offer stable and valid knowledge for all people at all times. This kind of Knowledge is not, therefore, the effect of the encounter with the sensible objects, because these cannot offer anything beyond the doubtful and the probable. Knowledge does not come from outside the being but from inside, from participation of the soul in νοῦς.

On the other hand, accumulation of erudite notions regarding the changeable phenomena of the sensible leaves the individual as he is, and contributes nothing to the removal of metaphysical ignorance (*avidyā* for *Vedānta*). However much may we understand the working mechanisms of the phenomenal (*māyā-avidyā* for *Vedānta*), however much material media may be invented to offer to the restless and unsatisfied "ego", it will remain as unsatisfied as ever. Sensory knowledge, in all the variety of its expressive modes, does not bring wholeness, it does not bring serenity, it does not bring authentic Knowledge, which is the source of fullness-bliss.

Empirical or sensorial knowledge may bring us the consolation of technicism, of consumerism, of dizziness by objects, but it can not bring us stable *pax profunda*.

«Even if we were to bring our sense intuition up to the highest level of clarity, we would not draw any closer to the nature of objects in themselves. So, we shall never

---

[1] Plato, *Politéia*, VII, 518. Op. cit. [Italics ours].

be able to know fully anything but our mode of intuition, our sensitivity, and this always in conditions of time and space originally inherent in the subject; but, no matter how illuminated our knowledge of their phenomena - which is all we are given of them - what objects in themselves might be remains unknown to us»[1].

Knowledge that does not have its roots in the inmost realm of being itself is alienated knowledge, and Plato, having *seen* and *comprehended*, in order to enable us to rediscover ourselves, does not address himself to fruitless opinion but to noetic Knowledge, the source of revelation of Being itself or of "what one is".

Kant launched a strong attack on the world of opinions, concluding that what we can know is at best nothing more than empirical representation based on sense experience; we can know the «simple modifications or foundations of our sensory intuition: but the transcendental object remains unknown to us»[2].

To know this latter we need a type of knowledge that does not spring from an experiential relation, but from a pure *intuition* which is *a priori* . Plato says that in the soul there exist *cognitive faculties* and *instruments* which are capable of comprehending-knowing the *in-itself*.

The being is not cut off from the context of the universal intelligible (Plato, as we have seen, did not postulate an absolute and irreducible duality), it is simply *oblivious* due to its freedom and capacity of assimilation with the sensible world. Identification with the sphere of "shadows" (myth of the cave) leads to disowning and excluding the

---

[1] Kant, *Critique of Pure Reason*, Part I, section II, 8. Laterza. Bari. [Italian Edition].

[2] *Ibid.*

noetic reality: the Idea; and hence the Supreme Good, or metaphysical One.

The second factor upon which rests the solution of human conflict, derives from the fact that, if man desires a better world, if he wishes to shape positive events, he must also know *how to contemplate the archetypal world so as to bring the sensible into as great a conformity with the intelligible as possible*; therefore he bears immense responsibility on the existential plane in which he lives. If on this plane things do not proceed as they should it is because the individual does not know how *to build* according to the laws of ideal Harmony (let us remember that above the doorway of Plato's Academy there was an inscription which read: «If one is not a Geometer he may not enter»; and Plato's is an ideal Geometry).

Man is a second Demiurge whose task is to bring the intelligible into the sensible and the sensible into the intelligible. This world is in ruins because man wishes it so, but it could be different if he strove with humility first to discover his internal Ruler and then *to contemplate* what is perfect at certain levels of being. His metallization has produced such a scissure as to create duality. The human being should operate in accordance with his most immediate archetype: the Demiurge or universal Intelligence. He is a prototype of the universal intelligible; he is a microcosm created on the model of divinity; that which the universal Intelligence accomplishes at the suprasensible level, man as particularized Intelligence - repeating, with due proportion, the demiurgic action - must create on the level of the sensible. Just as the architect must first intuit the model to be built, then draw the architectural geometry in a unitary synthesis, and finally mould the matter in conformity with the projected model; so must the architect-man first contemplate-intuit the ideal universal Model, then draw his architectural geometry according to the laws of Harmony, and finally mould the bodies, the compounds, to the greatest possible extent in conformity with the Model contemplated (see *Politéia*).

He should not do anything but *contemplate* the models, the paradigms and "materialize" them upon the plane of the sensible so that this may become a world of Accord, Harmony and Rhythm.

Plato's message is, therefore, twofold: realization or remembrance (*anámnesis*) of what one really is; and, consequently, construction of the sensible world, in which one lives, in accordance with the ideal principial Model.

If one desires a better world, according to Plato, there is no alternative to the one presented above; every other way is destined necessarily to fail or may be considered as mere demagogy.

It is opportune to note that Plato assigns a precise ethical task to man: that of constructing in himself and in society Order, Harmony, Measure and Beauty. These terms have a precise connotation within Platonic Teaching and this fact must be kept in mind.

Plato does not remit to others (God, Messiah, Gods, etc.), nor does he defer to some other time-place our responsibility for self-realization and social development. He puts before us the possibility of finding ultimate Truth and the means by which to reach it.

To conclude we can say that Plato's Teaching is directed towards the following objectives:

a) Towards the world of the metaphysical Comprehensive-Whole (Sphere of the supra-intelligible);

b) Towards the world of the noumena or of the archetypes (Sphere of the intelligible);

c)   Towards microcosmic individual, for his knowledge, his harmonious development and his happiness;

d) Towards society - as organized community - for right cohabitation and for right legislation and administration.

The first objective is the fruit of Realization of identity.

The second is the outcome of pure noetic contemplation.

The third objective is achieved through a work of purifying or rectifying our consciousness and the individuated psychological compound (the irascible and concupiscible Soul); this is the work of ascesis, of awakening to one's essential nature, of knowledge of what one really is.

Therefore Plato's is a philosophy for a high ethical realization which culminates in identity with the supreme Good. A further implication - and we must always insist upon this to avoid misunderstanding - is the aim for which Plato philosophizes is not mere conceptual skill for its own sake, but the transformation of man and of society.

The fourth objective can be achieved by building a State which is not the outcome of sectarian or absolutist manipulations, but a model of the universal Order. And for the implementation of this Plato does not take an abstract or theoretical stand, but formulates a complete body of legislation (see for example *Politéia* and *Laws*) capable of modelling the State, and therefore society, on the paradigm of the Idea. The principles of this legislation - obviously with appropriate adaptations of a practical nature - are valid even for today's society.

But there is more: Plato calls for the realized philosopher not to abstract himself from the society in which he lives - even though he may also do so, depending on his aptitude - but to become its Lawmaker and Ruler. This also implies that his Teaching, speaking in terms of *Vedānta*, includes different types of *mārga* (way-path): from *Jñāna* (knowledge-gnosis), to *Bhakti* (Eros-love), to *Karma* (right action). In fact we note that different Neo-platonic philosophers insist upon one or other aspect of his Doctrine. Plotinus, one of the greatest of the Neoplatonic philosophers, concentrated particularly on the aspect of knowledge-gnosis. Platonism, then, - speaking still in terms of *Vedānta* - addresses itself to the *brāhmaṇa*-priest and to the *kṣatriya*-lawmaker.

Thus Plato's philosophy, being an extraordinary and profound codification of the one perennial Teaching is highly operative, that is constructive; and if He places Reality beyond the contingent and the ephemeral, he does so not in order to pursue his own point of view, but to offer to the individual drugged by the movement of the "shadows" this incontrovertible evidence: that in the phenomenal-relative sphere there are no *constants*.

And the paradox is this: many "systems" of philosophy and science be they positivist, materialist or rationalist, etc., while claiming to be "realist" and certain of the discovery that man and reality are expressions of transitory and fleeting materiality, appear to the critical and thoughtful mind to be nihilistic, reductive and solipsistic.

That rationalism which denies any principle of higher order and appeals only to rational reasoning, isolates itself from pure intellectuality (*noûs*), falling within the exclusive dominion of corporeal individualism. This split having been effected, it becomes natural to tend more and more towards the material and sensible, to the point of considering man, and indeed Reality itself, as a mere phenomenon, a molecular accident whose sole fate is that of losing himself in "nothingness". Under this perspective, the empirical being - believing to be an absolute on the universal stage - considers itself entitled to manipulate the substance and destroy the forms, to introduce the manipulative technology into the order of reality without any ethical direction and without comprehending that this entails a profound metallization of daily life. This inevitably implies a marked estrangement from suprasensible reality, where we would recognize ourselves as drops of the same ocean, respecting all forms which function - after our "fall" - as a springboard for our return to the primeval condition.

Plato, like Śaṅkara, does not propose acting in a disorderly manner for what regards the sensible, he does not indicate *doing* or, rather, the overdoing typical of the irrational and lacking entity, but develops a philosophy of *how to Be really*.

Any action not supported by pure noetic intellectuality or not subject to the Idea as the ontological principle; or again, the mere sensorial sensible not connected with the universal principle cannot but run into its own destruction.

One may say that there are philosophies of becoming and philosophies of Being; Plato, placing himself beyond dogmatic partiality, proposes a philosophy of the *Whole*, of Totality, the very same philosophy that Śaṅkara proposes with the *Advaita Vedānta*.

That the Teaching of Plato is at once a philosophy and a realizational "mysticism" is beyond all doubt. But precisely because it presents these characteristics, it requires a special predisposition of the intellect, particularly in the present era, permeated by materialist, relativist and phenomenalist positivism, yet extremely reductive and incapable of explaining the totality of Being, of pointing out a universal dimension to man in conflict.

Although two thousand four hundred years have passed, Plato's Teaching, like that, more ancient, of the *Veda*, still

exists and will continue to exist because it belongs - beyond all the indefinite interpretations which may arise out
of culture or erudition - to that *Philosophia perennis* which
is above and beyond time and space.

We may conclude these brief notes on Plato with the
Prayer of the Philosopher:

«Phaedrus: ...But let us go, the heat of the day has
diminished.

- Socrates: Ah yes, but would it not be proper to offer
a prayer to the gods before setting out?

- Phaedrus: And why not!

- Socrates: Oh dear Pan, and all ye other Gods that
dwell in this place, fill me with inner Beauty, and let what
is outside be harmonious with what is inside; may I regard
the wise as rich and have only that amount of gold that the
man of moderation can carry with him. Is there anything
else to ask, Phaedrus? For me the prayer is in conformity
with right measure.

- Phaedrus: I am one with you in this prayer, since
among friends all is held in common.

- Socrates: Let us be going»[1].

---

[1] Plato, *Phaedrus*, 279 b-c. Op. cit.

RAPHAEL

Unity of Tradition

Raphael, who has attained a synthesis of Knowledge (not to be confused with eclecticism nor with syncretism), aims at "presenting" the Universal Tradition in its many Eastern and Western expressions. He has spent a substantial number of years writing and publishing books on the spiritual experience; his works include commentaries on the *Qabbālāh*, Hermeticism and Alchemy. He has also commented upon and compared the Orphic Tradition with the works of Plato, Parmenides and Plotinus. Raphael is also the author of several books on the pathway of non-duality (*Advaita*), which he has translated from the original Sanskrit, offering commentaries on a number of key Vedantic texts.

With reference to Platonism, Raphael, in this very book, has highlighted the fact that if we were to draw a parallel between Śaṅkara's *Advaita Vedānta* and a Traditional Western Philosophical Vision we could refer to the Vision presented by Plato. Drawing such a parallel does not imply a search for reciprocal influences, but rather it points to something of paramount importance, a sole Truth inherent in the doctrines (teachings) of several great thinkers, who although far apart in time and space, have reached similar and in some cases even identical conclusions.

One notices how Raphael's writings aim to manifest and underscore the Unity of Tradition, under the metaphysical perspective. This does not mean that he is in opposition to the dualistic perspective, to the various religious faiths, or "points of view".

An embodied real metaphysical Vision cannot oppose anything, and what counts for Raphael is the unveiling through living and being, of that degree of Truth which one has been able to contemplate.

It is in the light of the Unity of Tradition that Raphael's writings and commentaries offer the reader's intuition precise points of correspondence between the Eastern and Western Teachings. These points of reference are useful for those who want to address a comparative Doctrinal study and to enter the spirit of the Unity of Teaching.

For those who follow either the Eastern or the Western traditional line these correspondences help in comprehending how the *Philosophia Perennis* (Universal Tradition), which has no history and has not been formulated by human minds as such, «comprehends universal truths that do not belong to any people or any age». It is only for lack of "comprehension" or of "synthetic vision" that one particular Branch is considered the only reliable one. From this position there can be but opposition and fanaticism. What degenerates the Doctrine is sentimental, fanatical devotionalism as well as proud intellectualism, which is critical and sterile, dogmatic and separative.

In Raphael's words: «For those of us who aim at Realization, it is our task to get to the essence of every Doctrine, because we know that as Truth is one, so Tradition is one even if, just like Truth, Tradition may be viewed from a plurality of apparently different points of view. We must abandon all disquisitions concerning the phenomenal process of becoming, and move onto the plane of Being. In other words: we must have a Philosophy of Being as the foundation of our search and of our realization»[1].

---

[1] Cp., Raphael, *Tat tvam asi* - That thou art. Aurea Vidyā. New York.

Raphael interprets the spiritual practice as a "Path of Fire". Here is what he writes: «...The "Path of Fire" is the pathway each disciple follows in all branches of Tradition; it is the Way of Return. Therefore, it is not the particular teaching of an individual, nor a path parallel to the one and only Main Road... After all, every disciple follows his own "Path of Fire", no matter which Branch of Tradition he belongs to».

For Raphael it is important to express through living and being the truth that one has been able to contemplate. The expression of thought and action must be coherent and in agreement with each being's own and specific *dharma*.

After more than thirty-five years of teaching, both oral and written, Raphael is now dedicating himself only to those people who wish to be "doers" rather than "sayers", according to St. Paul's expression.

Raphael is connected with the *matha* founded by Śrī Ādi Śaṅkara at Śṛṅgeri and Kāñcīpuram as well as with the Rāmaṇa Āśram at Tiruvannamalai.

Founder of the Āśram Vidyā Order, he now dedicates himself entirely to the spiritual practice. He lives in a hermitage connected to the *Āśram* and devotes himself completely to a vow of silence.

* * *

May Raphael's Consciousness, expression of Unity of Tradition guide and illumine along this Opus all those who donate their mens informalis (non-formal mind) to the attainment of the highest known Realization.

GLOSSARY

Advaita Vedānta: (*darśana*) non-dual or metaphysical view of reality codified by Śaṅkara.

Anámnesis: remembrance, awakening to the reality of the intelligible, of what one really is.

Aparavidyā: secondary, relative knowledge, Lesser Mysteries.

A priori: "prior to (empirical) experience"; innate.

Arché (ἀρχή): archetype, suprasensible "model", principle.

Ātman: the true Self, identical to *Brahman*.

Avidyā: metaphysical ignorance, unawareness of one's own true nature.

Bhagavadgītā: "The Song of the Blessed One", a synthesis of Teaching and a spiritual guide for all of Humanity. It is considered the Gospel of Hinduism.

Brahman: Being, the Substratum of all "appearances", Absolute.

Causa sui: lit. "its own cause"; that which does not depend on anything for its existence.

Chóra (χώρα): undifferentiated "matter", the substratum of all forms both at gross and subtle levels.

Darśana: philosophical perspective or "point of view". In Hindu philosophy, six are the *darśana* based on the *Veda-Upaniṣad*.

Diánoia: a grade of knowledge of the intelligible. It refers to mathematical and geometrical aspects.

Dóxa (δόξα): opinion, a grade of knowledge, knowledge of the sensible world.

Epistéme: "Science-knowledge" of the intelligible; it includes "rational knowledge" (*diánoia*) and "pure intellection" (*nóesis*).

Epoptéia (ἐποπτεία): the highest Initiations into the Mysteries.

Idea (ἰδέα): being, real being; essence. Also *eidos* (εἶδος).

Intelligible (or suprasensible) world: supraindividual, beyond the world of names and forms. Universal dimension.

Logos: reason, the rational principle (as opposed to feeling).

Māyā: "movement that produces forms". The projective and veiling principle that makes all things appear. For a full discussion on *māyā*, cf. Raphael's *The Pathway of Non-Duality*. English translation by Motilal Banarsidass, Delhi (India).

Metánoia-periagogé (μετάνοια-περιαγωγή): "conversion".

Nóesis (νόησις): intellection, pure understanding of the Ideas and of the absolute Principle. Knowledge of the "thing in itself".

Noetòs (νοητός): intelligible.

Noûs (νοῦς): the noetic mind; Intelligence, Intellect; universal Soul.

Oratòs (ὁρατός): that which can be seen, visible.

Orphism: Branch of Western Tradition, the very root of western metaphysics, philosophy and spirituality.

Ousía (ουσία): idea-essence.

Paravidyā: supreme knowledge, Greater Mysteries.

Philía: friendship among those who love Knowledge, who are in search of the Divine.

Philosophy of Being: the philosophy which has as its object pure Being or Reality in itself beyond all phenomenal becoming.

Polis: city-state; nation, in modern terms.

Politéia: constitution or form of government. Title of one of the most important Dialogues of Plato, usually translated as "Republic", though it covers all forms of government.

Prakṛti: matter, *chóra*, substance out of which all things are made.

Ṛg Veda: one the sacred books of Hinduism. Inspired hymns, containing the seeds of the highest forms of knowledge and spirituality known to man.

Samādhi: state of union with the Divine or one's own transcendental consciousness (Self/*ātman*); contemplation.

Saṁsāra: becoming; the perennial succession of birth, life, death and rebirth.

Śaṅkara: one of the greatest philosophers of ancient India (788-820 A.D.), codifier of the *Advaita Vedānta* (metaphysics of Non-duality, of Vedic inspiration), a most decisive answer to the philosophical and existential problems of Being and non-being, One and many, Absolute-Being and relative-becoming, etc.

Sensible world: the phenomenal world of forms.

Summum Bonum (tò agatón, τὸ ἀγαθόν): the Supreme Good. The platonic One-Good, the One of Plotinus, Absolute.

Theoria (θεορία): inner contemplation.

Turīya: the Fourth or non-qualified (*nirguṇa*) *Brahman*; Absolute; metaphysical Being, it corresponds to the One-Good of Plato.

Vedānta: lit. "end of the *Veda*" both in the sense of scope and final part; Branch of the Eastern Tradition based mainly on the teaching of the *Upaniṣad*. It may also mean "Upaniṣad" because these form the concluding part of the *Veda*.

PUBLICATIONS

Books by Raphael
published in English

The Pathway of Non-duality,
Advaitavāda
Motilal Banarsidass, Delhi

Pathway of Fire,
Initiation to the Kabbalah
S. Weiser, York Beach, Maine, U.S.A.

Essence and purpose of Yoga,
The Initiatory Pathways to the Transcendent
Element Books, Shaftesbury, U.K.

Initiation into the Philosophy of Plato
Shepheard-Walwyn (Publishers) Ltd., London

The Threefold Pathway of Fire
Aurea Vidyā, New York

At the Source of Life
Aurea Vidyā, New York

Beyond the illusion of the ego
Aurea Vidyā, New York

Tat tvam asi, That thou art,
The Path of Fire According to the Asparśavāda
Aurea Vidyā, New York

Orphism and Initiatory Tradition, Raphael
Aurea Vidyā, New York

Other Publications
in English

Māṇḍūkyakārikā *, Gauḍapāda
The Māṇḍūkya Upaniṣad with the verses-*kārikā* of
Gauḍapāda and commentary by Raphael.
Aurea Vidyā, New York

Ātmabodha *, Śaṅkara
Self-knowledge
Aurea Vidyā, New York

Self and Non-Self *
The Drigdriśyaviveka attributed to Śaṅkara
Kegan Paul International, London

Forthcoming Publications
in English

Vivekacūḍāmaṇi *, Śaṅkara
The Crest-jewel of Discernment

Five Upaniṣad *
Īśa, Kaivalya, Sarvasāra, Amṛtabindu, Atharvaśira

The Bhagavadgītā *

The Regal Way to Realization, Yogadarśana *, Patañjali

Beyond Doubt, Raphael

Aparokṣānubhūti *, Śaṅkara
Self-realization

The Science of Love, Raphael

* Translated from the Sanskrit and commented by Raphael